# Pacific educators speak:
# Valuing our values

# Pacific educators speak: Valuing our values

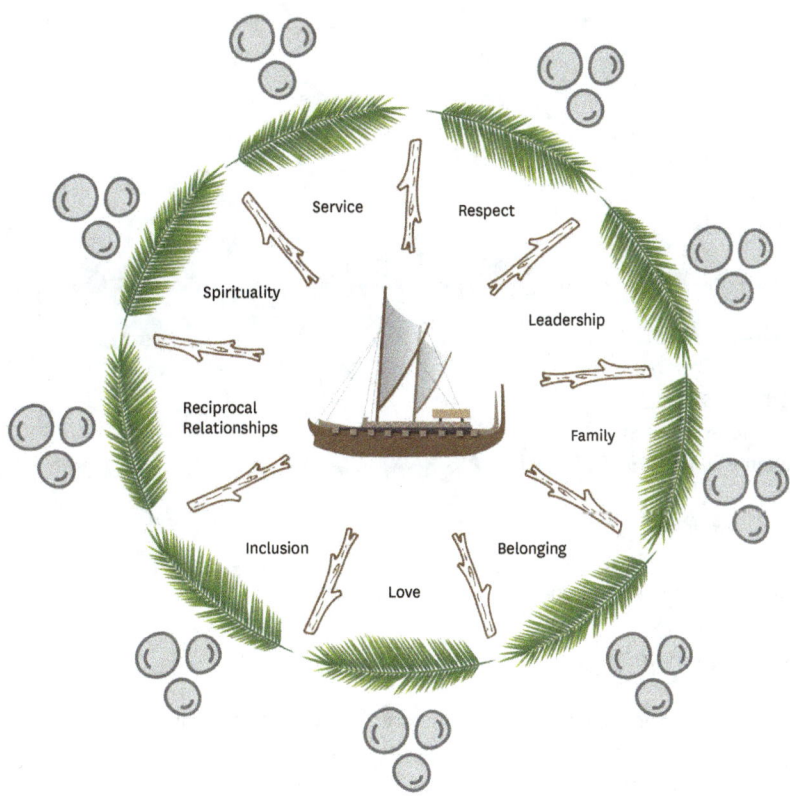

Fuapepe Rimoni,
Ali Glasgow, and Robin Averill

*O au matua o fanau*
*Children are our treasures*

The book is dedicated to the forebears of Pacific children who have safeguarded, carried, and nurtured languages and cultural knowledge through the generations and to our children who carry these forward and are the beauty of the Pacific.

NZCER PRESS
Level 4, 10 Brandon St,
Wellington

www.nzcer.org.nz

© Fuapepe Rimoni, Ali Glasgow, and Robin Averill, 2022

ISBN 978-1-99-004052-8

No part of the publication may be copied, stored, or communicated in any form by any means (paper or digital), including recording or storing in an electronic retrieval system without the written permission of the publisher.
Education institutions that hold a current licence with Copyright Licensing New Zealand may copy from this book in strict accordance with the terms of the CLNZ Licence.

A catalogue record for this book is available from the National Library of New Zealand.

Designed by Smartwork Creative

**Cover image:** Rangisani Tim Glasgow

## Tatalo āmata

*Tātou ifo ma tatalo*
*Let us bow and pray*

*Lo mātou tamā o i le lagi*
*Our father in heaven*

*Ia pa'ia lou suafa, e pa'ia lava oe tamā*
*We worship you in your name*

*Mātou te fa'afetai i lou alofa ma tausiga ia'i mātou,*
*fa'afetai mo le ola ma le mālosi aemaise lenei mafutaga, fa'afetai*
*We thank you for your love, care, and strength towards us all,*
*particularly our fellowship, thank you*

*Le Atua e, fa'amagalo i matou pe afai, ua le atoatoa*
*se matou galuega ua fai*
*Lord, please forgive us for any wrongdoing*

*Fa'amanuia nai o matou fanau o le Pasifika o lo'o feagai ma*
*aoaoga, foai le poto, foai le loto matala latou te tauivi ai*
*Bless all the Pasifika children, who are learning, give them the*
*wisdom and heart to work hard*

*Fa'amanuia le galuega a Faiaoga uma, ia latou maua fo'i le poto*
*mai i lau afio e faatino ai o latou tiute ma latou tofi*
*Bless the work of our teachers, shower them with your wisdom*
*to do the work they have been chosen to do*

*Le Atua e, e leai lava se mea matou te mafaia pe a aunoa ma oe*
*Heavenly Father, we are nothing without you*

*Afio mai, ma mafuta mai I lenei fo'i aso ma*
*fuafuaga uma o le a feagai ai*
*Be with us as we prepare ourselves for our daily duties*

*O le tatalo lea o ou tagata e ala atu ia Iesu le faaola*
*This is our prayer through Jesus Christ*

*Amene*
*Amen*

*Sifaga Valerie Rimoni*

# Acknowledgements

We are sincerely grateful to all the educators who shared their thoughts with us and enabled the writing of this book. Thank you very much also to The Honourable Luamanuvao Dame Winnie Laban for graciously providing the inspiring foreword. We are indebted to all of our wonderful values navigators who have provided their thoughts to begin the values chapters: Matiti Tokelau Akoga Kamata, Hutt Valley; the Niuean Early Childhood Community, Māngere; Te Punanga o Te Reo Kuki Airani, Wellington; Malo Sepuloni, the A'oga Amata, Newtown; and Dr Tanya Wendt Samu, Dr Rae Siʻilata, Associate Professor Kabini Sanga, and Dr David Taufui Mikato Faʻavae.

Rangisani Tim Glasgow, we are delighted with the Pacific values compass for the cover and many thanks to Taʼase Pusa for your very useful literature searching. Thank you to Joanne Averill-Rocha for the initial ideas for implications for practice and to Associate Professor Fiona Ell, Lynda Knight-De Blois, Kadin Good, Dr Carolyn Tait, Cushla Thomson, Wills Dobson, Janice Shramka, Chris McIntyre, Diane Wiechern, and Josh Allen for your very valuable feedback on drafts of the book. This book was only an idea when we first spoke with David Ellis at the New Zealand Council for Educational Research and we are very grateful to David for his encouragement, inspiring ideas, and support which have helped transform the idea into a reality.

Our gratitude to Te Herenga Waka – Victoria University of Wellington for support which enabled the study and this book.

To you all: Meitaki maʼata, Faʼafetai lava, Malo ʻaupito, Fakafetai lahi lele, Fakaue lahi, Vinaka, Tankiu Tumas, Mauruuru, Mahalo, Māuruuru, Ko rabaʼa ko bati n rabaʼa, Faiak seʼea, Kia ora and Very Warm Pacific thanks.

# Foreword

Talofa lava, Malō e lelei, Ni sa bula vinaka, Kia orana, Talofa ni, Taloha ni, Faka'alofa lahi atu, Kam na mauri, Talofa, Gud de tru, Halo olgeta, Ia orana and warm Pacific greetings.

Economist Adam Smith argued in the 18th century that the "dead hand" of tradition holds back economic progress and that traditions and cultures have no part in education. We now recognise that Pacific Island cultural values and practices can be a great strength for our children and young people and that our culture and traditions can be the living heartbeat of our educational institutions and programmes.

Belonging, family, love, service, spirituality, reciprocity, respect, leadership, and inclusion are the nine values that this volume, *Pacific Educators Speak—Valuing our Values*, is structured around. Each chapter focuses on one value and includes the words of Pacific educators talking about their experiences and how they apply their values to their practice. Discussion questions, extra reading, and practice suggestions are provided for further exploration and as a teaching resource.

Fuapepe Rimoni, Ali Glasgow, Robin Averill, and all the Pasifika contributors to this volume are to be congratulated on developing, producing, and contributing to this research- and data-based publication. I also acknowledge the contributions of the New Zealand Council for Educational Research, and Te Herenga Waka – Victoria University of Wellington for their support. Fa'afetai tele lava.

Infusing early childhood, primary, secondary, and tertiary education programmes and institutions with Pacific Island cultural values and training our educators to celebrate the cultures and traditions of the children, families, and communities they serve, will ensure that our values are lived and are more than just talk.

Ia manuia.

**Luamanuvao Dame Winnie Laban QSO, DNZM**
*Assistant Vice-Chancellor (Pasifika),*
*Te Herenga Waka – Victoria University of Wellington*

# Contents

Chapter 1: Education for Pacific heritage learners in New Zealand ................1
Chapter 2: Belonging..........................................................................................16
Chapter 3: Family...............................................................................................35
Chapter 4: Love .................................................................................................52
Chapter 5: Service .............................................................................................67
Chapter 6: Spirituality........................................................................................79
Chapter 7: Reciprocal relationships .................................................................97
Chapter 8: Respect ..........................................................................................109
Chapter 9: Leadership .................................................................................... 129
Chapter 10: Inclusion ...................................................................................... 143
Chapter 11: Honouring Pacific values: A compass for educators ................ 159

Chapter One

# Education for Pacific heritage learners in New Zealand

Malō e lelei, Talofa lava, Taloha ni, Talofa ni, Kia orana, Fakaalofa lahi atu, Tālofa, Ni sa bula vinaka, Halo olaketa, Ia orana, Aloha, Kam na mauri, Halo, Kamawir Omo, I'orana, Namaste, Mālō, Kia ora, Very warm Pacific greetings! A very warm welcome to this book!

*Feliuliuakiga o te au mo he lumanaki taua o fanau*
*Recognising the moving currents for the sustainable future of our children*

*Our very warm thanks to the Tokelauan community of Matiti Tokelau Akoga Kamata, Hutt Valley for sharing this proverb to help open the book.*

> Looking after Pacific children's needs is a daily challenge for Pacific educators. We have to be strong advocates for our Pacific children and families to ensure they know they belong in their educational setting. Our cultural practices are often overlooked in curriculum and teaching; however, these are important for being ourselves and are vital to our community. We all need to work together to dismantle what is problematic in our education system for Pacific people. Everything non-Pacific educators can do to support Pacific educators and Pacific children and families is valuable.

These words highlight that every educator can and must make a positive difference for their Pacific learners and colleagues. In this chapter, we explain why our focus is on how values important to many Pacific people can help understand how to make this positive difference. We describe the policy and theoretical context of Pacific education in New Zealand and the values within this, and the study that enabled us to collect the educator voices we are sharing here. We explain the metaphor we are using to frame the ideas in the book and the content and design of the chapters that follow.

**Why focus on values?**
Understanding Pacific values and integrating these into teaching, learning, and learning environments is critically important for Pacific learners' learning and wellbeing (Fletcher et al., 2009; Pene et al., 2021; Surtees et al., 2021; Theodore et al., 2018). Pacific values are fundamental to our education policy which demands improvement in educational opportunities for Pacific heritage learners; however, there are varied interpretations of the values amongst Pacific and non-Pacific heritage people (Averill et al., 2020). Those working in our early childhood centres, schools, and tertiary educational contexts need practice consistent with Pacific perspectives of the values for Pacific heritage learners to thrive. To support educators to work effectively with Pacific learners and their families and bring what works for many Pacific learners to the fore, each chapter of this book presents a range of perspectives from Pacific educators on a value important to them and their communities. Views and experiences are drawn from Pacific educators across early childhood, primary, secondary, and tertiary education. As the majority of these views and experiences can be used to inform practice across educational sectors, they are presented together rather than being separated by sector.

Deeply considering these educators' perspectives helps us understand ways of creating learning environments that can enhance Pacific learners' sense of identity, wellbeing, and achievement, and the purposes of education. The perspectives shared in this book show that demonstrating and nurturing the Pacific values in learning environments is likely to enhance communication amongst all involved in the learning process, important for supporting learning. Given the growing proportion of Pacific heritage people throughout New Zealand society, the perspectives shared are relevant to all educators and learners in New Zealand, whether or not there is a high proportion of Pacific learners within their immediate learning context.

While education policy refers to nine Pacific values (belonging, family, love, service, spirituality, reciprocal relationships, respect, leadership, and inclusion), neither the policy nor associated resources delve deeply into how the values are considered, lived, demonstrated, or nurtured by Pacific people or how these can be enacted in educational contexts. Our research has explored Pacific educators' perceptions of these values and how they can be embedded within practice in our Eurocentric education system, one that places strong emphasis on responsiveness to Te Tiriti o Waitangi. We are respectful of the place of tangata whenua and Te Tiriti o Waitangi within education in Aotearoa New Zealand and share understandings of the learning of Pacific heritage people within this context.

There are many components, practices, and processes that can contribute to teaching that is highly suitable for Pacific learners. Including learning experiences relevant to and drawn from learners' lives and communities, using pedagogies that inspire, motivate, and nourish Pacific learners, and involving Pacific families and communities within learning environments are all examples. We have focused on exploring perceptions of the values in our work because understanding of these can inform consideration of how each of these components, practices, and processes can be incorporated in learning programmes in ways comfortable for Pacific learners and their families and conducive to maximising learning and wellbeing.

### The Pacific Values Compass

The opening thought of this chapter, *Feliuliuakiga o te au mo he tumanaki i taonga o fanau*, helps us think about the context we are travelling in when we navigate ways to work with Pacific learners and their families. We need to understand the currents well and know how to manoeuvre using these to help power our voyage. Pacific people are descendants of explorers, discoverers, and innovators who used their knowledge to traverse distant horizons using the currents, winds, and stars. These ancestors viewed the world as a "sea of islands", rather than "islands in the sea" (Hau'ofa, 1993, p. 7), emphasising the relationships between the people who lived on the islands and their lands, rather than the geography and great distances between them. To provide some historical context, beginning from 3,000–4,000 years ago, travel around the Pacific was used for trade, marriage, visiting relatives, adventure, and engaging in conflict. People sailed from Southeast Asia, via Indonesia, Borneo, the Moluccas, Melanesia, Papua New Guinea, Solomon Islands, Vanuatu, and Fiji. They settled in Tonga and Samoa around 1500 BC. There, the Polynesians developed and settled into using a social structure of districts, each headed by an Ariki (Ali'i, E'iki, Haka'iki). Under the Ariki, administration was carried out by royal clan chiefs and lesser chiefs (identified in Rarotonga as Rangatira and Mataiapo respectively). Pacific people spread eastward on Te Moana Nui a Kiwa (Iva, Hiva, Iwa) to the Cook Islands, the Society Islands, Marquesas, Tuamotu, Rapa Nui (Easter Island), Hawaii, and Ao Tea Roa (New Zealand) (Davis, 1999).

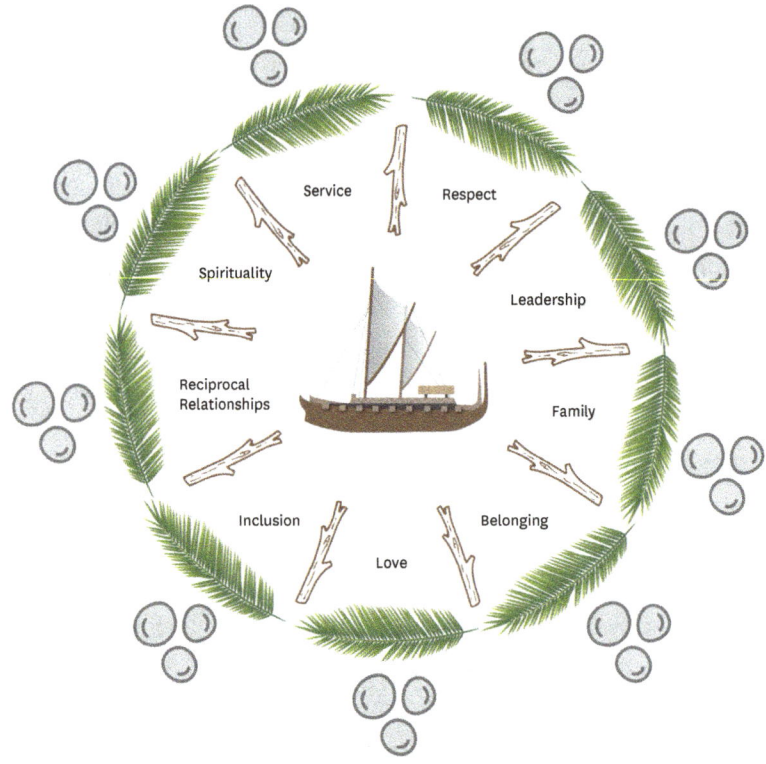

Figure 1  Pacific Values Compass

Figure 1 shows our version of the Satawal Atoll star compass, a compass used in an ancient navigation system based on observations of the sea, winds, wave patterns, bird migrations, and sky (Howe, 2006). The Satawal Atoll star compass is being used again in the recent revival of Pacific Ocean voyaging and metaphors have long been associated with this compass. Stones, coconut leaves, and banana trunk fibres are used to make the Satawal Atoll star compass—the stones represent the rising and setting positions of the stars and constellations, the coconut leaves represent the eight swells used in steering, the banana trunk fibres running across the circle represent the reciprocal relationships of rising and setting points of stars and constellations, and the vaka in the centre helps learners visualise the star paths (Howe, 2006).

In our version of the compass, the Pacific Values Compass, we encompass the diverse range of educational provision and relationships in Aotearoa New Zealand. Each coconut leaf symbolises one of the Pacific values. Beside each leaf are the three guiding stones that we use to symbolise the learner, the educator, and the parent—representing the triadic interactions and relationships between them for learning. The coconut leaves illustrate the ways in which the value is demonstrated and nurtured, and the banana trunk fibres the interrelationships between the values and the connections between people. Each aspect of the compass is important for navigating what makes for excellent educational opportunities for Pacific learners.

We focus on the essence and behaviours associated with each value separately. Each chapter of this book focuses on one coconut leaf—one value—and what makes for educational practice and environments that are rich in demonstrating and nurturing the value. However, just as all parts of a compass are needed to understand navigation, the values are intertwined, and many practices demonstrate and nurture more than one value. The interdependence of the values is evident in the chapters. In the final chapter, we consider four further values also important to many Pacific people and how attending to all the values holistically can assist educators think, act, and foster the wellbeing in educational settings of our Pacific children and families.

**Where have our Pacific families come to New Zealand from?**

By 2028, it is expected that around 17% of New Zealand learners will have Pacific heritage (Ministry of Education, n.d.). There are three racial heritage island groups of New Zealand Pacific learners: Polynesia (Samoa, Tonga, Tokelau, Cook Islands, Niue, New Zealand Māori, Tuvalu, Rotuma, Tahiti, Hawaii, Marquesas); Melanesia (Fiji, Solomon Islands, Vanuatu, New Caledonia, Papua New Guinea); and Micronesia (Guam, Republic of Kiribati, Federated States of Micronesia, Nauru, Northern Marianas, Palau, Marshall Islands) (Kalavite, 2020).

Each Pacific island nation has its own distinctive ways of living, beliefs, cultures, languages, and identities. Despite this diversity and complexity, the terms "Pacific" and "Pasifika" are used fairly generically within education policy in New Zealand to encompass people who enjoy heritage from one or more of many Pacific nations—including those who have recently arrived in New Zealand and those who have been in the country for generations. There is a danger that understandings of Pacific people's identities, experiences, priorities, beliefs, and ways of being and doing are seen generically rather than for the beauty of the differences between people who originate from specific islands and island groups (Kalavite, 2020; Pene et al., 2021). While this book focuses on values seen to be fairly commonly held across many Pacific people (Ministry of Education, 2013, 2018), readers are encouraged to see nuances and differences in perspectives between people both within and across island nation groups.

**Education policy**

There has been increased emphasis over recent years on supporting Pacific learners within our education system and increased responsiveness from policy makers to Pacific voices, giving hope that the education system can be developed in ways that align with the aspirations of Pacific people (Wendt Samu, 2020). The *Pasifika Education Plan 2013–2017* (*PEP*) (Ministry of Education, 2013) sets out the strategic vision for improving Pacific education outcomes through increasing responsibility and accountability for these and outlining aspirations for enhancing economic growth and social wellbeing. Pacific learners, parents, families, and communities are central within the *PEP*, which aims for closer alignment between learners' home, cultural, and educational environments so that communities, education providers, and services can work together towards better outcomes.

Following the *PEP*, The *Action Plan for Pacific Education* (2020-2030) (*APPE*) (Ministry of Education, 2020) describes the vision of ensuring "diverse Pacific learners and families are safe, valued, and equipped to achieve their education aspirations" (p. 4). Key focus areas include working reciprocally with diverse Pacific communities to respond to unmet needs, confronting systemic racism and discrimination in education, enabling every educator to become culturally competent, partnering between families and educators in designing education opportunities, and increasing our numbers of highly competent educators of diverse Pacific heritages.

A compass metaphor focuses a resource for supporting educators' implementation of the *PEP* and *APPE*, *Tapasā* (Ministry of Education, 2018)—tapasā being the Samoan term for compass. Nine values central to the *PEP* and *Tapasā* were the focus of the research that led to research informing this book. *Tapasā*, as does Pacific education policy more widely, discusses education for Pacific learners in generic ways, rather than highlighting differences by heritage nation. For the views presented in this book, we follow suit, and unless the participant has done so in their statements to us, we do not identify participants' heritage nation/s.

Pacific language nests, first established in New Zealand in the 1980s, provide an inter-generational language and culture-based approach to early childhood education, language maintenance, and community building (Glasgow, 2019). Pacific language nests provide programmes that encompass cultural practices and protocols and use music, mat time, and other learning experiences to provide language learning opportunities. The nests are a hub for their Pacific community, and grandparents and elders play a significant role in providing cultural knowledge, understanding, and leadership. There are around 50 Pacific language nests in New Zealand, each nurturing the language and culture of Samoa, Cook Islands, Niue, Tonga, or Tokelau. Originally established to cater for children just from these nations, many language nests now host children from many heritage countries. Many Pacific language nests were established for a particular purpose at a particular time and, while their philosophy still remains, for many the policies, expectations, and funding models established by the Ministry of Education have made it increasingly difficult to stay true to the philosophy (Glasgow, 2019). For example, some Pacific language nests were originally set up as play group-style get togethers where the grandparents would come in for a few hours, bringing their mokopuna. Now the funding model requires that they are full-day education and care, and many centres are multicultural because they have had to widely recruit families to attend. Having an authentic Pacific programme is becoming increasingly difficult for some nests. Sadly, many centres have closed since they were set up in the early 1980s.

**Theoretical perspectives**

Our research processes have been framed by two Pacific-based theoretical models to help us maximise the integrity of the study, the quality of the study data, and our responsiveness to participants. Firstly, the Vaka or Va'atele framework (Glasgow, 2019; Si'ilata, 2014; Si'ilata et al., 2018) uses the metaphor of a double-hulled canoe that traverses the ocean to encourage understanding of the importance of using learners' linguistic and cultural resources within curriculum learning. This framework helps illustrate how Pacific learners can be encouraged to learn and thrive within connected school, family, and community relationships and settings that prioritise knowledge learners bring to the learning setting and connections between the knowledges of their home and learning settings. This metaphor aligns well with our book's metaphor of the guiding Pacific Values Compass, in that educators' understanding of the compass—the Pacific values—can set their learners' vaka on a correct, safe, enriching, and successful journey.

The second guiding framework for our research is the Fale tele (meeting house) model, which represents key values as poutu of a fale (Luafutu-Simpson, 2011). The structures that comprise the fale represent alofa (love and commitment), tautua (service and responsibilities), and fa'aaloalo (respect and dignity)—factors important to the overall health and wellbeing of a Pacific person. The fale represents a safe environment that provides a sense of belonging and spirituality. The family within the fale provides a strong foundation of love, belonging, and relationship-building. The poutu remind us of the importance of developing characteristics, traits, and behaviours that support individual learners and their communities. By using these two models, we place cultural aspects central to academic, social, environmental, economic, and spiritual effects on learners' health and wellbeing. The models both serve to emphasise the crucial role of family and community in relation to these effects and help us realise that multiple interrelated factors are important for educators to consider in creating learning environments that can maximise our Pacific learners' wellbeing and learning.

Our research processes have been guided by Pacific research methodologies, which prioritise holistic perspectives of knowledge and scholarship, oral communication practice, and protocols of consensus and respect (Anae et al., 2001). Scholarship within Pacific contexts involves using research approaches that honour Pacific protocols, values, and etiquette, which we have prioritised in our project; for example, through service, reciprocal relationships, and respect.

**Calls from literature**

A wide range of literature calls for educators to know and understand their learners well, forge effective partnerships with learners' families and communities, and strongly embrace and draw from learners' cultural identities; however, many learning settings are not yet catering as well as possible for Pacific learners (Ministry of Education, 2019). Excellent guidelines for practice are available to educators including in *Tapasā* (Ministry of Education, 2018) and the *Best Practice for Teaching Pacific Learners: Pacific Evidence Brief 2019* (Ministry of Education, 2019). Our aim is not to recreate similar work, but to share voices and practices consistent with the calls from literature and policy groups from Pacific educators in our study.

**Our research**

Over 30 Pacific educators from across educational setting types and across three urban centres have been involved in our 4-year research study, all having given fully informed consent to participate. Some have contributed understandings across all values and others for some of the values. We interviewed the educators about their perceptions of the focus value and how they demonstrated and nurtured the value in their teaching. For most, the interviews were held one-to-one, and, for others, a talanoa-style discussion was held. All interviews and discussions were recorded and transcribed. We observed the teaching of most educators, recording examples of the target values in teachers' practices and interactions and across the learning environment. We draw, in the main, from the interview data in this book, with an example of practice provided in each chapter to illustrate the perspectives shared. In the wider study, interview and observation data were also collected from non-Pacific educators across sectors and locations. While the data from non-Pacific educators has informed our thinking about the values, it has not been drawn from in this book on Pacific educator perspectives.

We approach this work from our experience of working with student teachers, teachers/educators, and teacher educators, two of us with Pacific heritage (Fuapepe, Samoan and Ali, Cook Island and Tahitian) and one without (Robin, New Zealand European). Collectively we have experience teaching in early childhood, primary, secondary, and tertiary teaching contexts. As educators, we each bring our own understandings to how we interpret values and what may be needed to enact these, drawing from our own background and experiences. Together we have explored answers to the research questions: What do Pacific values mean to Pacific children and families? How can learning environments strongly embody and nurture these values?

In previous writing from this work, we have described Pacific perspectives of the Pacific values of respect (Rimoni & Averill, 2019), service (Rimoni et al., 2021), policy supports and challenges (Averill & Rimoni, 2019), and how perceptions of these values can differ between Pacific heritage and non-Pacific heritage people (Averill et al., 2020). Here we share perspectives of the Pacific educators in our study and glimpses of their teaching from our lesson observations. We use these educators' words to outline factors important for living the Pacific values that all educators can use to enhance the achievement and wellbeing of our Pacific learners. The chapters that follow indicate that rethinking, reforming, and reacting are key at all educational levels and in all aspects of our education system to ensuring the Pacific values can be experienced and nurtured and provide ideas for moving forward.

## Reading this book

The views opening each chapter have been kindly gifted by invited "values navigators"—all Pacific heritage education leaders with deep insight into Pacific ways of knowing, doing, and being. Key themes about the focus value from the literature and participants are described next. Most of each chapter is dedicated to our participants' words, curated and softly edited for flow, to ensure they represent what we heard from participants and, consistent with ethical requirements of the research, to ensure participants and others cannot be identified. The perspectives and practices shared in the body of each chapter are drawn from many Pacific educators from around Aotearoa who work daily with Pacific learners, people from a diverse range of Pacific communities. We summarise key ideas from the chapter by linking back to the value navigator's contribution, then each chapter concludes with discussion questions, ideas for further reading, and practices that can help demonstrate and nurture the target value.

## Engaging with the educators' perspectives

We hope the chapters will be used for self and group reflection and development. Please engage with the perspectives shared. For example, before reading each chapter, ask yourself:

Tahi *What does this value mean to me?*
Lua *How do I demonstrate this value in my actions within and outside of education?*
Tolu *Which teaching strategies and behaviours strongly demonstrate and nurture this value?*

As you read, ask:

Fā *What are similarities and differences between the views I am reading and my own?*
Lima *What might Pacific learners and their families expect in relation to how the value is enacted by educators and within learning settings?*
Ono *What do teaching and learning look like when this value is strongly embedded?*

Fitu  *How will I strongly demonstrate and nurture Pacific perspectives of this value in my teaching and interactions?*

We encourage readers to listen to the Pacific educators, learners, and families in their own learning context and to add further examples suitable for their own learning context to the practice summaries for each value.

**Summary**

A substantial and increasing proportion of New Zealand learners have Pacific heritage but the proportion of Pacific heritage educators, across all sectors, is much lower than this, with most New Zealand educators non-Pacific. Ideally, all Pacific heritage learners can be themselves in learning environments that strongly support their academic achievement, identity, and wellbeing. Understanding Pacific values well can help educators ensure their teaching is suitable for Pacific learners and their families, as explained by one of our Pacific educators:

> Educators can demonstrate respect by being open to learning and immersing themselves in understanding the cultural space. This may mean moving outside their comfort zone. As Pacific people, we've had to do that, and we've taken on a lot of Western ways. So, one way of showing respect for Pacific people is for teachers to live in the Pacific space, to go and find out about this. You can't achieve authenticity and meaningful relationships until you've experienced things from another point of view, so teachers can demonstrate respect through looking for and using those opportunities to really find out about Pacific people's life experiences, by spending time in the Pacific community. When teachers build up this knowledge, they can pull on those ideas respectfully when they're working with students.

The perspectives shared in this book can help us all understand what makes for suitable teaching and learning environments for learners from Pacific nations. While there are commonalities within and across groups, there are also differences to which educators can become attuned to help ensure that in our learning environments our Pacific learners and their families can always feel they belong and are included, can enjoy the sense of family, can experience love and be spiritually nourished, can enjoy service and leadership opportunities, and can expect and consistently experience respectful reciprocal relationships. This is our ideal. The Pacific Values Compass, guiding proverb, and Vaka and Fale tele models can be used as tools by educators aspiring to be great educators of Pacific learners. We hope this book will motivate and inform educators on their journey and that the currents empower their travels, alongside our Pacific and non-Pacific learners and fanau, to ensure that all may have positive and enriching futures.

## References

Anae, M., Coxon, E., Mara, D., Wendt-Samu, T., & Finau, C. (2001). *Pasifika education research guidelines*. Auckland UniServices. https://www.educationcounts.govt.nz/publications/pasifika/5915

Averill, R., Glasgow, A., & Rimoni, F. (2020). Exploring understandings of Pacific values in New Zealand educational contexts: Similarities and differences among perceptions. *International Education Journal: Comparative Perspectives, 2*, 20–35.

Averill, R., & Rimoni, F. (2019). Policy for enhancing Pasifika learner achievement in New Zealand: Supports and challenges. *Linhas Críticas, 25*, 549–564. https://doi.org/10.26512/lc.v25.2019.23780

Davis, T. (1999). *Vaka: Saga of a Polynesian canoe*. University of the South Pacific.

Fletcher, J., Parkhill, F., Fa'afoi, A., & O'Regan, B. (2009). Pasifika students, teachers and parents voice their perceptions of what provides supports and barriers to Pasifika students' achievement in literacy and learning. *Teaching and Teacher Education, 25*(1), 24–33. https://doi.org/10.1016/j.tate.2008.06.002

Glasgow, A. A. H. (2019). *Ko toku reo ko toku ia mana: My language, my identity—The Pacific language nest: How language, culture and traditions are supported and promoted for the Pacific communities of the Cook Islands, Niue and Tokelau in Aotearoa New Zealand*. Unpublished PhD thesis, Victoria University of Wellington.

Hau'ofa, E. (1993). Our sea of islands. In E. Waddell, V. Naidu, & E. Hau'ofa (Eds.), *A new Oceania: Rediscovering our sea of islands* (pp. 2–16). School of Social and Economic Development, University of the South Pacific.

Howe, K. R. (Ed.). (2006). *Vaka Moana: Voyages of the ancestors: The discovery and settlement of the Pacific*. Bateman.

Kalavite, T. (2020). Toungāue cooperative pedagogy for Tongan tertiary students' success. *Waikato Journal of Education, 25*(1), 17–29. https://doi.org/10.15663/wje.v25vi1.783

Luafutu-Simpson, P. (2011). *Exploring the teaching of effective approaches for assessing young children's learning in early childhood centres: Developing an authentic Samoan lens*. Ako Aotearoa.

Ministry of Education. (n.d.). *Pacific education briefing for the incoming minister*.. https://www.beehive.govt.nz/sites/default/files/2020-12/Pacific%20Education%20BIM.PDF

Ministry of Education. (2013). *Pasifika education plan 2013–2017*. https://assets.education.govt.nz/public/Documents/Ministry/Strategies-and-policies/PasifikaEdPlan2013To2017V2.pdf

Ministry of Education. (2018). *Tapasā: Cultural competencies for teachers of Pacific learners*. https://teachingcouncil.nz/assets/Files/Tapasa/Tapasa-Cultural-Competencies-Framework-for-Teachers-of-Pacific-Learners-2019.pdf

Ministry of Education. (2019). *Best practice for teaching Pacific learners: Pacific evidence brief 2019*. https://www.educationcounts.govt.nz/publications/pacific/best-practice-for-teaching-pacific-learners-pacific-evidence-brief

Ministry of Education. (2020). *Action plan for Pacific education 2020–2030*. https://www.education.govt.nz/our-work/overall-strategies-and-policies/action-plan-for-pacific-education-2020-2030/

Pene, F., Taufe'ulungaki, 'A. M., & Benson, C. (2021). *Tree of opportunity: Re-thinking Pacific education*. University of the South Pacific Institute of Education.

Rimoni, F., & Averill, R. (2019). Respect: A value vital for Pasifika learners. *Set: Research Information for Teachers*, (3), 3–11. https://doi.org/10.18296/set.0146

Rimoni, F., Averill, R., & Glasgow, A. (2021). Service: A deep, meaningful value vital for Pasifika learning. *Set: Research Information for Teachers*, (1), 12–19. https://doi.org/10.18296/set.0192

Si'ilata, R. (2014). *Va'atele: Pasifika learners riding the success wave on linguistically and culturally responsive pedagogies*. Unpublished PhD thesis, University of Auckland.

Si'ilata, R., Wendt Samu, T., & Siteine, A. (2018). The Va'atele framework: Redefining and transforming Pasifika education. In E. A. McKinley & L. T. Smith (Eds.), *Handbook of Indigenous education*. https://doi.org/10.1007/978-981-10-1839-8_34-1

Surtees, N., Tufulasi Taleni, L., Ismail, R., Rarere-Briggs, B., & Stark, R. (2021). Sailiga tomai ma malamalama'aga fa'a-Pasifika—Seeking Pasifika knowledge to support student learning: Reflections on cultural values following an educational journey to Samoa. *New Zealand Journal of Educational Studies, 56*, 269–283. https://doi.org/10.1007/s40841-021-00210-7

Theodore, R., Taumoepeau, M., Tustin, K., Gollop, M., Unasa, C., Kokaua, J., ... & Poulton, R. (2018). Pacific university graduates in New Zealand: What helps and hinders completion. *AlterNative: An International Journal of Indigenous Peoples, 14*(2), 138–146. https://doi.org/10.1177/1177180118764126

Wendt Samu, T. (2020). Charting the origins, current status and new directions within Pacific/Pasifika education in Aotearoa New Zealand. *New Zealand Annual Review of Education, 26*, 197–207. https://doi.org/10.266686/nzaroe.v26.7138

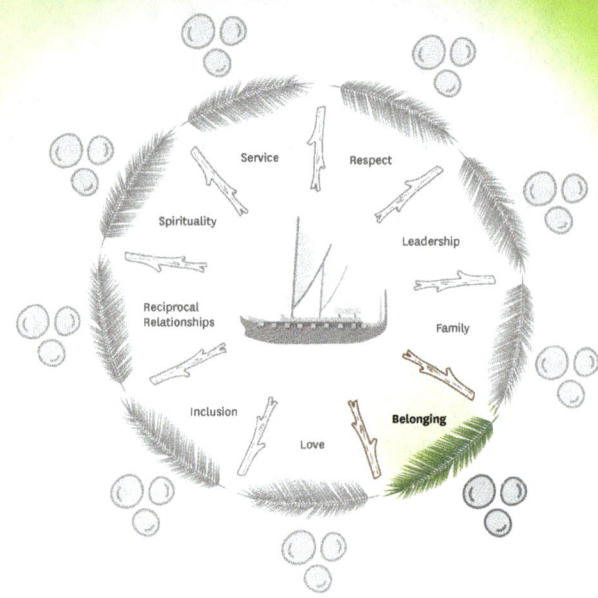

Chapter Two

# Belonging

**What does belonging mean to Pacific people? How can learning environments strongly embody Pacific perspectives of belonging?**

*Ke fakamanatu e tau taoga mo e tau taleni he tau mamatua*
*Promote and retain the traditions and knowledge of the ancestors*

*This statement, shared with Ali Glasgow on her thesis journey, is included here with much gratitude and love to the Niuean Early Childhood Community in Māngere, Auckland, for the statement and for their guidance in developing an understanding of a sense of belonging to Niue, gained by Ali on her journey. Ali shares thanks also to Ianeta Ikiua, "my Niuean Early Childhood Education Mentor and Tuakana, who guided me so graciously in my quest to learn about the beautiful Niuean people, traditions, language and culture". Fakaaue lahi, to one and all.*

- Everyone feeling a strong sense of belonging is fundamentally important to many Pacific people.
- Children confident they belong are more likely to have a strong sense of who they are and to learn well.

- Parents feel they belong in the learning community, centre, and classroom when they are warmly welcomed, and their ideas and questions are understood and prioritised.
- Teachers can ensure Pacific children feel belonging by aligning learning environments with their out-of-school interactions, expectations, and practices and ensuring that what children bring to their learning and can offer others is appreciated.
- Belonging is nurtured by warm, open, respectful interactions that acknowledge strengths and skills, and by consistent, predictable practices and ways of interacting.

A strong sense of belonging in relation to the learning environment can contribute to Pacific learners' academic identity and achievement (Mayeda et al., 2014; Rimoni, 2016). Learners' own feelings of cultural identity, seeing their culture reflected in their learning environment, and identifying with others within this environment with shared traditions and belief systems can contribute to learners' feelings of belonging (Nakhid, 2003). Belonging impacts on comfort, wellbeing, and our capability and desire to share ideas and activities (Maslow, 1968). For Pacific learners, feeling belonging includes feeling wanted, being and doing things as part of a group, being able to talk with anyone and push yourself, and feeling belonging results in feeling happy, safe, comfortable, connected, and laughter (Rimoni, 2016). This chapter illustrates that "belonging" means much more than "I need to make sure Pacific children feel welcome here".

Let's hear from our Pacific educators …

## What does belonging mean to you?

Belonging is a concept easier for most to get their head around than some of the other Pacific values, in the sense of "What does it mean to belong for a child? for a community?" There has to be a connection from the home to the educational setting. There has to be some feeling for the child of "I can understand this place", and "I can identify myself in this place". This connection could be around interpersonal connections and the practices that the child observes the teacher using; it could be the environment—how this looks, sounds, and feels—and it could be temporal, such as in how time is used and how well this fits with Pacific perspectives of time. Belonging is important because it helps children feel a strong sense of identity.

Belonging in a Samoan family is often related to what everyone's contributions are to the family and community. We know what everyone is good at and that everyone's got something to offer, so when you go to family gatherings or community events, people know you for a particular skill and they will say, "Hey, can you do this because we know (or we've heard, or we've seen) you do this, and you do a pretty good job." So, belonging for us, in terms of family and community outside of school life, is about everyone having something to contribute for the greater good. Belonging is tied up with service and leadership as well. It is always connected to how you can better serve your family, how you can better serve your community. Your family represents your community. Pacific people, especially those arriving for the first time in New Zealand, connect with other Pacific people through the church, where they identify village and other community connections. It is here where a sense of belonging and identity are developed through service to community.

Belonging means Pacific children and parents being able to be honest and open with the teacher and not feeling a power differential. There will always be a power issue in the minds of many Pacific parents because we look to teachers as trained professionals who are going to help our children to get a qualification—there'll always be that sense of respect. Many Pacific teachers try to make the power difference less obvious. Teachers need to show parents, "We value what you bring", to have learning environments where all our children feel belonging and thrive.

### *What are learning environments that ensure belonging for Pacific children and parents like?*

These learning environments are places where Pacific children experience, see, and hear things from their culture and background. They have photographs and maps of Pacific places and people on the walls, beautiful Pacific crafts in the room, Pacific music playing, displays that include

Pacific languages. They are places where singing and whole-group tasks are used to teach and learn while nurturing a sense of community, shared experience, and togetherness. They are places where you hear Pacific hymns and prayers in Pacific languages and where Pacific children give thanks for the new day of learning. They are places where Pacific songs, legends, and dances are included in the class curriculum. They are places where parents are welcome to share their expertise and passions. They are happy, cheerful places full of humour and acceptance where Pacific children are comfortable, positive, enthusiastic about learning, support one another, and feel they have a place and can have a say. We run whānau competitions throughout our school and those emphasise the importance of belonging and being together, of looking out for one another and participating together.

### Example in practice: Starting the day with a lotu

The children of the Samoan language unit know the day starts with lotu. They sit ready, in class lines, arms folded, legs folded, facing the children whose turn it is to manage the readings and prayers. Teachers, teacher aids, and parents sit on chairs at the sides and at the back and, as visitors, we sit with them. There are cuddles and encouragement for children. The large room had tapa cloth, large photos of children of the unit in traditional clothing and with special artefacts and other Samoan artwork and treasures. There are Bible readings, prayers, and singing that everyone joins in, led by the children, all in Samoan. Children who come late are acknowledged by the closest teacher, shown where to put their bag and slip into place on the sides of the group. The lead teacher welcomes everyone and talks about things that have happened over the weekend—it was Mothers' Day. She shares her experiences and asks the children to share theirs. Humour is included, 'It wasn't Fathers' Day!' Notices of the day are given, and children are told of visitors to the unit. They are asked to turn to the back to face us and we were invited and welcome to speak and explain why we were visiting with them. Finishing up included lua pati, two claps and all being told to 'Have a blessed day'.

This starting protocol ensured the day started with giving thanks for the new day, acknowledging their faith in God's presence in their learning, and created a sense of belonging for all. It was a time to remind children of the values expected from them throughout the day, such as being respectful and showing love to each other. All knew what was expected and how to participate. Everyone prayed together and sang together. Everyone was welcomed, events happening in their lives were acknowledged, and the shared experience, held in a special place with special people—all of their teachers—began the school week. This way of starting the day enabled us to see many values in practice—belonging, respect, leadership, inclusion, spirituality, family, and love.

In learning environments suitable for Pacific learners and parents, the teacher notices, recognises, and acknowledges each person. They accept everyone with the same priority. They see the potential of each learner and go out of their way to support, encourage, and uplift learners. They are deliberate about using inclusive practices to make sure all feel their learning space is fair, safe, non-biased, and equitable. For example, I always feel that the course I'm teaching belongs to me, but it's a partnership with the students that I'm working with. They contribute to the course because I prioritise establishing relationships and giving them space to talk and share because, to me, belonging is about making that space where learners feel that they can open up. I'm clear and consistent in my expectations of their participation. I encourage Pacific people to share. They show they belong by talking, by feeling safe to share their thoughts, by moving to different spaces in the room, and sitting with different people.

> *belonging is about making that space where learners feel that they can open up.*

Educators need to make sure all children feel equally privileged. The school and tertiary systems don't always allow that to happen, so it's challenging to do this without going above and beyond their usual work. Equity doesn't mean doing the same for each child but doing the appropriate thing for each child. For example, my niece knows Samoan dance and certain cultural roles so well that she's become our cultural expert of dancing in our family gatherings, teaching the other children—because our aunties and our uncles see her as someone who enjoys that part of the culture. She knows for herself that she belongs because she has something good to offer that she can share. She doesn't just go every day to just sit there and watch; rather, she feels, "Oh, I've got something to offer. I know I belong here because I can give something", and she's keen to get the next opportunity to give this experience, help, and support to others.

### *How can teachers ensure learners feel a strong sense of belonging in the learning environment?*

Learning environments we are part of do not always give us a sense of belonging. We live in a society founded on a treaty, but responsiveness to the treaty is not enough to help Pacific people feel belonging. Until teachers achieve the sense for Pacific children that, "This place is for me", the child's never going to be able to achieve as readily as those who naturally feel part of the education system. Children having a strong sense of "who I am" and strong pride in themself can be challenging for teachers to achieve, because identity is not seen as important as other traits by many in the classroom and education system. It's tricky for many Pacific children because many learning situations can set them up with a mixed understanding of who they are as people in that, they can feel that to be a person in this world, they have to give away so much of who they are that they don't want to give away. They either choose to, or choose not to, or somehow manoeuvre through so they can feel comfortable in non-Pacific settings—but why should it be that so many Pacific children have to give away so much to achieve academically?

As Pacific people, we are respectful, we are humble. We put other people in front of us. People in learning environments need to be like this for Pacific children to feel belonging. Education is key to how children view themselves, and teachers have that huge responsibility to nurture learning for all children—it's not just about reading, writing, and content—it's about everything that creates a sense of belonging. Noticing body language, like the clearing of the voice, comes into how Pacific people notice and realise how to act in each setting. When practices we are used to are not used in the learning environment, Pacific people can feel that there are different signals that they can't grapple with. As a Pacific person, I'm constantly thinking, "Oh my gosh, how do I fit into this setting?"

In the meantime, the teacher can have moved on to something different. Teachers need to be attuned to children having to work out how they are expected to behave to their teachers, which can be very different from how they behave with adults at home. For example, their teacher might say, "You show me, look at me", while the child thinks, "But I got a clip across the ear because I looked at my father—he said, 'Don't look at me, that's bad manners', and now I'm told by my teacher to look at him, eyeball him?" That's totally conflicting for the child. Such differences take a lot of energy and getting our head around, so teachers can mistakenly assume, "Well, this child isn't engaging", but the teacher instead could explore how the child is most comfortable to interact.

*What knowledge and understanding of Pacific people, experiences, cultures, and priorities are important for educators to have to help ensure Pacific learners feel belonging in their learning environment?*

It's hard for many non-Pacific teachers to know what would be ideal for them to know. It's easier for teachers not to be responsive to the lives of their Pacific learners, especially as they may not have been in Pacific settings. It can be easy for them to think, "Well, this is the way education works. If you want to succeed, you've got to just do it like this." However, teachers need to know that underneath what they see on the surface is everything that Pacific children and families experience and bring with us, that is often deeply ingrained. Pacific people did not leave all their ways of being and interacting behind when they came to New Zealand. We're all from different island groups and we hold on to that sense of our own special place in the Pacific. Children come with a rich understanding of their own place because that's our whakapapa. They know the songs, stories, protocols, and the recipes of these places, and how the songs and stories are used. We call it turangavaevae, in Cook Islands Māori—in Aotearoa it is turangawaewae—we have a strong connection back to our own place, and our sense of belonging back to our own places is something teachers need to know about and understand for each Pacific child. With each child who comes with a Pacific background, part of their pride is from being able to connect back to their Pacific heritage, to their place. Teachers need to realise there are nuances and protocols around these things. These nuances are complex, because within each Pacific nation behaviours and expectations differ. For example, I understand that in Samoa, vā is practised very much with a hierarchy, so that we understand who's the most important, and we give them more vā, more space. Educators need to understand to use different strategies for different children. One-size-fits-all is just not how we work as Pacific people. We are very diverse—diversities include how many family generations have been living in New Zealand. Some may be more enculturated into a Western way of living than others. Regardless of our background in New Zealand, we all have to straddle both Pacific and Western worlds.

I probably represent a model of where we're moving to in our Pacific communities because, in my family, there's a lot of intermarriage, not only between the Pacific Island groups but between Pālagi, our Papa'ā, and Pacific as well. We're having to grapple with a sense of, "Well, I work in two worlds, but my heart is in this space, and I don't want to forget that I am very proudly Pacific." Teachers need to understand that there's a range of ways of thinking about belonging that our Pacific children bring with them and are sensitive to. Teachers need to achieve a sense of understanding for each individual child, through getting to know them and their family groups, getting to know what their family aspirations are for their children, and not seeing anything as a deficit. Teachers need to act fairly, with every child's sense of belonging equally important. Teachers must do their very best to make sure that they have a strong connection with each child so that Pacific children and their families do have a sense of belonging.

Back in our home countries, we work, we educate, we teach. Children learn alongside their more able older brothers and sisters in a sort of apprenticeship model. We learnt as an apprentice, alongside Dad out in the plantations or fishing or wherever. Many educational settings here don't offer the same amount of scaffolding as these situations do. Here, children are encouraged to be independent and individual problem solvers. Many Papa'ā children can do very well in this way of learning because they've been raised in these ways. The model doesn't fit so well for many of our Pacific children who haven't, so teachers need to provide many ways of learning so that all children can learn well and feel belonging. I think I saw quickly, "Okay, I have to be and learn like an individual, so this is what I'll do." My siblings weren't like that—they found it difficult, and it is so unfair—they're far more intelligent and able than I am, but the education system didn't cater well enough for them. That's still the case for Pacific learners now—it is very unfair.

Educators and their learners would benefit from teachers broadening their own horizons. Educators need to think beyond their classrooms, to think broadly about the community they serve, and be more a part of Pacific community groups. Doing this will help with all kinds of understandings—like, what is it like being part of a Pacific community group? or sitting at church for a long time? or not being able to understand the language you are immersed in? Being in such situations would help educators understand how uncomfortable it can be when we go into a situation where we don't understand the language, where the protocols are very different to those we are used to, where the hierarchy plays out in ways we might not expect or understand, where we are not sure who to listen to, and where we do not know how to read body language. Such experiences can give some insight into how it might be for Pacific people coming into a Western, English-medium learning environment, as these are the kinds of things many Pacific people grapple with in our education system on an ongoing basis.

> *Educators need to think beyond their classrooms, to think broadly about the community they serve, and be more a part of Pacific community groups.*

It can be hard for educators to ensure children and parents feel belonging if they do not know about their experiences. Very sadly, many Pacific families suffer effects of poverty. Education can fall easily into place for children in families with a professional background. It is often very different for many of our Pacific children, whose parents may be factory workers or currently unemployed—the daily battle of making sure that the bills are paid and there's enough food takes a lot of energy, and helping your children navigate the education system at the same time can be very difficult. It may be that the family are currently living in a garage. Children might not be able to get to a library, or, if they do get there, they may have to be home to look after younger siblings or cook dinner because Mum and Dad are doing the night shift. Not many educators have been to the Ministry of Social Development with their Mum and Dad and had to wait in line to see them get a benefit. Not many have been to the food bank or felt the guilt at having to go back again because their family is large and there are many people to feed. Not many have family who have broken the law and may be in prison. These are experiences that many educators don't think about that some children bring, but we have to make sure to nurture children in these situations to feel belonging in our learning environments. Pacific people with family in these situations take them as a usual part of life. We have a deep sense that they're still family, we're connected even though they have acted in ways that may not be part of the mainstream establishment. They are part of us, and we accept them. We can't not accept them because that's who we are. Educators need to be sensitive to Pacific children in these situations. Educators seeing such challenges as deficits can hinder children having a true sense of belonging.

We have an open-door policy where we have parents come in and interact with children, which comes into that sense of belonging. It enables that connection amongst everyone. This helps build that relationship with the parents and the community.

*How important is it to notice and reject negative race-based perceptions for creating learning environments that engender belonging?*

Negative race-based perceptions completely undermine feelings of belonging. When you live in the Pacific world you know that race-based perceptions and racist comments and critique are sadly prevalent. I have siblings who look strongly Polynesian, so I know exactly what this racism and lack of celebration of difference can be like, how it can manifest. Since I look less Polynesian, I've also seen the other side of it, but I know that negative dialogue and discourse, unconscious bias, and unchallenged views exist. They might be hidden, but they appear every so often. We encounter racism all the time. How on earth are our children ever going to have a sense of belonging when we have that pervasive racist discourse that surrounds us? Teachers need to focus on the strengths and advantages people offer and recognise and set aside any negative preconceived ideas, prejudices, and perceptions of disadvantage about Pacific people. For example, educators should make no judgements about capability based on spoken English—in their communities these same people can be leaders. They could be part of an ariki family—they may be matai.

As educators, we need to look at the systems and expectations that are in place in learning environments, even everyday things such as expectations around being on time, completing homework. We need to challenge and change those that are inherently racist because they are set up for a particular way of viewing the world, but don't work well for all. Unfortunately, most of our learning environments privilege certain ways of working, doing, and being. Educators need to be empathetic and understanding, like thinking, "OK, they haven't done their homework. Well, actually they don't have anywhere to do their homework, so I need to help provide a place for that here, or I can't expect it." When I think about how much we've had to give away to be part of this education world, it makes me sad. I'm thinking of my family who've moved here and others who have moved as migrants into low-paying jobs, and all the associated effects of these moves, because they wanted a better life. The education system they came for has in many cases only educated them to a certain degree, so that they are only able to work as cleaners, factory workers and similar jobs. I think there's still a bit of a legacy of the feeling in society that, "Well, they are part of society. Shouldn't they be grateful? How dare they try and aspire to be more?" I like to think that our educators have moved on from that type of thinking, but there's still a legacy of it in society and education.

> *Unfortunately, most of our learning environments privilege certain ways of working, doing, and being.*

Many educators and Pacific children and parents will have some uncertainty about each other, caused by growing up in different worlds. For example, if a non-Pacific educator draws from Pacific contexts in their teaching, the child or parent might think, "What are the motives of this person?" or think, "They come from another background, so why are they trying to do that?" or have a concern that a relevant cultural protocol is not understood. Similarly, an educator might wonder why a child or parent is acting in a particular way, "Why is she going overboard? I'm not used to that kind of reaction", or ask themselves, "Have I done something wrong?" Ideally, the educator needs to bring the whole classroom together, have discussions that develop relationships and understanding, and establish an environment where children or parents who may have other points of view can comfortably voice them. If this isn't done, some will form the view that there is no place for their perspectives in the learning environment and a sense of belonging will not be able to develop. Education needs to move more towards those kinds of dialogues being commonplace and expected.

I think of my grandson who's 12 and probably very Polynesian in the way he works and operates. He often is having detentions and other punishments at school. Most of his mates are the Māori and Pacific boys in his group. I despair because he'll probably leave school as soon as he can because he just doesn't like it; he doesn't get it. It is the teachers' and the school's responsibility to ensure he feels he belongs there, but they have not achieved this. The school has got a Māori term for detention. I said to the family, "What the heck is that?" I asked, "Well, do they have a Māori word for getting a merit as well?" Perhaps I have heightened sensitivity to things like that, but he's another one who's not going to aspire to achieve in education, simply because he is more Polynesian in his way of thinking and looking. Education and qualifications are not the be all and end all, but it does help you to get a better job and a better income, and not having a sound education perpetuates the disadvantage for this child and their children in turn.

Educators need to be able to unpack, dismantle, and disrupt what they're doing to see how they can make sure that no child loses their sense of who they are. I think there's a lot of learning around what a sense of belonging can be for each individual child. Teachers need to take the time, using that sense of vā if they want to use it. They need to know who each child is, what makes them tick, and adjust their classroom practice to accommodate each learner. They need to make sure they don't get too far ahead of each child in their teaching, so that no one is left behind, and no one can think, "I'll never catch up, I'll never get there. This place isn't for me." Children and parents can read attitudes in teachers' body language. When teachers see confusion, or that they've left someone behind, they need to backtrack to bring everyone along together.

### *What perspectives about "time" are useful for educators to have?*

I've worked in the Pacific and in some of the more remote islands where the notion of time is very different to New Zealand society's ideas. As a Pacific person, I work in a different way in relation to time than my non-Pacific colleagues and my institution expects—except that I have to fit with a timetable that isn't always working for my students or me, which can be stressful. It would be good to build the sense of wellbeing and flow that can occur when we're not always managing by the clock into teaching practices. There are practices related to time that enhance the sense of belonging for Pacific children—it could be just noticing and adopting aspects of how we manage our day. It can be educators giving their time generously to others. It can be ensuring children who may be a few minutes late to class because they have to run an errand for the family knowing this is okay and that they are not going to be penalised. Children's sense of belonging is enhanced when they know the educator understands that, at times, they need to do something for their family. Similarly, belonging is helped for learners when there's flexibility around assignment submission when they are carrying out responsibilities to the family.

### *Are more Pacific educators needed for Pacific learners to feel belonging?*

I like using everyday things and hands-on experiences linked to our children's home country of Niue to help develop a sense of belonging because the children are taking in everything else at the same time as they are doing the learning. It's all for making a sense of belonging. This is who we are. This is what they see. It's us. For the parents as well, this approach gives them a sense of belonging. They know they have brought the children to the right place. They're getting the best opportunity to learn about Niue and their culture here. Using the language is also building the sense of identity for those children. Whether the child is Samoan or Tongan, we use the Niuean language because the words are similar across the languages. Children are becoming almost trilingual, learning Niuean, Samoan, and Tongan because they are all in the same language family which is lovely. It really is.

Pacific teachers understand our children better than non-Pacific teachers. I want more Pacific teachers. In some earlier research on educational transitions, I explored what some parents of Pacific early childhood children wanted from their child's school. Many looked to the schools which had Pacific teachers because they felt that in these schools at least these teachers would have an idea of their expectations as Pacific parents. They felt that, even if the teachers didn't come from their own home nation, they would know something about Pacific ways, and they felt more confident that they would be able to talk to those teachers, and that those teachers would understand them. It seems like there always will be challenges for Pacific children and parents in education until we address the imbalance of who is in our teaching workforce. Until we have more teachers from a Pacific background, Pacific children and families feeling belonging in our education settings is going to be a battle.

There will be non-Pacific people who will say, "We don't want our child to have a Pacific teacher. She's not going to cut the mustard. She hasn't been through what we know. She hasn't been to piano lessons and ballet classes and extra maths tuition. How can she adequately teach my child?" Some children are very advantaged in learning settings—their background aligns with Western approaches to learning. They know how things work and what is expected. Many of the parents of these children have been through our learning environments themselves, so they know how they work. It's a very difficult road for the teacher to manoeuvre around all these different groups within a very diverse classroom and help everyone feel strong belonging—but that's the job. I recall one of my capable non-Pacific students saying, "Well, I think our Pacific children are not achieving so well because they don't have experiences to draw from", and I'm thinking, "Well, yes they have." Educators don't have to have come from a Pacific background to create a place of belonging for Pacific learners—they can develop and use cultural understandings to help ensure Pacific children and parents belong.

*Do you have any final thoughts about the Pacific value of belonging?*

Pacific children already belong. They want to learn and thrive. Everything educators can do to ensure a strong sense of belonging for Pacific learners and their families is important for enhancing these children's learning and life experiences.

In summary, attending to the value of belonging means promoting and retaining Pacific traditions. Consistency between the learning environment and the child's out-of-school experiences, being respectful, holding strengths-based attitudes in communication and interactions, valuing how time can be considered and experienced, and supporting our Pacific educator colleagues are all part of what is needed to establish belonging. People feel belonging when they feel known and understood and when they can contribute and be open and true to themself. Belonging is enhanced when protocols and practices important to you are used and respected and when family members are welcome and comfortable.

## Discussion questions

Taha  *What understandings and practices are necessary for creating learning environments that deeply value belonging?*

Ua  *How can educators learn about each learner to ensure belonging can be felt by each learner and their family?*

Tolu  *How can negative race-based perceptions be noticed, rejected, and avoided?*

Fa  *What will learning environments look and feel like when Pacific perspectives of belonging are strongly in place?*

## Ideas for extra reading

"You've gotta set a precedent": Māori and Pacific voices on student success in higher education

Mayeda, Keil, Dutton, & Ofamooni (2014)

Educational experiences of high-achieving Pacific learners in tertiary education are presented in this article. Supports and challenges learners face in relation to family, university support, role modelling,

Indigenous teaching and learning practices, racism, and colonialism are discussed. This study found that establishing a sense of belonging and social environment enhanced learners' motivation and achievement.

**Talanoa ako: Pacific talk about education and learning**
Fairbairn-Dunlop, Chu-Fuluifaga, Reynolds, Abella, & Rimoni (2021)

This extensive resource includes a detailed literature review of five main areas that Pacific parents, families, learners, and communities believe need further consideration for the educational achievement of Pacific learners to be well supported. Themes of belonging and family permeate the review as key factors of Pacific learners' wellbeing and academic success. The review frames partnership between educators and Pacific families as essential to ensure the ideas, knowledge, beliefs, values, and languages Pacific people bring are recognised and valued by educators and reflected in educator practice.

**Tama Samoa: Exploring identities in secondary school**
Rimoni (2017)

This article draws from the voices of tama Samoa secondary students and discusses complexities for tama Samoa in relation to their personal identities as they moved through their secondary schooling. Western and Pacific ideas of cultural identity are discussed. The perspectives from tama Samoa shared in this article help us understand that identity and a sense of belonging for Pacific learners in educational settings can be affected by the various worlds they occupy (i.e., family, peers, school, cultural or church groups), being able to be there for friends when needed, and not letting their friends or their family down.

**"Intercultural" perceptions, academic achievement, and the identifying process of Pacific Islands students in New Zealand schools**
Nakhid (2003)

This article discusses explanations behind the failure of New Zealand schools to ensure suitable academic achievement for Pacific learners. Teachers' and learners' perceptions of identity development and insights held of one another are discussed. The study found that, for Pacific learners, a sense of belonging connects with learners' cultural identities and lacking a sense of belonging was associated with lack of achievement.

## References

Fairbairn-Dunlop, P., Chu-Fuluifaga, C., Reynolds, M., Abella, I., & Rimoni, F. (2021). *Talanoa ako: Pacific talk about education and learning.* Ministry of Education. https://pasifika.tki.org.nz/Media/Files/Talanoa-Ako/Talanoa-Ako-Pacific-talk-about-education-and-learning

Maslow, A. (1968). *Toward a psychology of being.* Van Nostrand Reinhold Company.

Mayeda, D. T., Keil, M., Dutton, H. D., & Ofamo'Oni, I. F. H. (2014). "You've gotta set a precedent": Māori and Pacific voices on student success in higher education. *AlterNative: An International Journal of Indigenous Peoples, 10*(2), 165–179. https://doi.org/10.1177/117718011401000206

Nakhid, C. (2003). "Intercultural" perceptions, academic achievement, and the identifying process of Pacific Islands students in New Zealand schools. *Journal of Negro Education, 72*(3), 297–317. https://doi.org/10.2307/3211249

Rimoni, F. (2016). *Tama Samoa stories: Experiences and perceptions of identity, belonging and future aspirations at secondary school.* Unpublished PhD thesis, Victoria University of Wellington.

Rimoni, F. (2017). Tama Samoa: Exploring identities in secondary school. *New Zealand Annual Review of Education, 22,* 112–121. https://doi.org/10.26686/nzaroe.v22i0.4151

## Educator practice—Demonstrating and nurturing belonging

| My role | My actions |
|---|---|
| **Interacting with learners** | Be open-hearted and listen carefully. |
| | Learn about learners and use this knowledge to make the learning environment comfortable. |
| | Discuss expectations and co-construct learning goals with learners. |
| | Include cultural artefacts, posters, music, and other culturally linked activities in the learning environment. |
| | Include songs, greetings, legends, and traditions in the curriculum. |
| | Give of yourself. |
| **Interacting with parents and families** | Have welcoming face-to-face meetings with parents with time for useful discussions. |
| | Find out what you need to do to give each child a sense of belonging. |
| | Have language experts available for translating oral or written word. |
| | Send letters and surveys to explore cultural background of learners and their families. |
| | Keep communication with parents open with regular communication and information evenings. |
| | Discuss time frames and homework expectations. |
| | Establish/nurture a homework club. |
| | Attend Pacific functions you are invited to attend. |
| **Planning** | Find out the cultural groups represented in the class. |
| | Find out learners' favourite events and traditions and plan to celebrate them and Pacific Language Weeks, White Sunday, and other Pacific celebrations through the curriculum. |
| | Know about and build on what learners know and can do. |
| | Learn and teach using traditional songs, sayings, and games. |
| | Learn and use words from Pacific languages in day-to-day classroom practice, such as for transitions between learning experiences, praise, and encouragement. |
| | Enable learners to work in subgroups according to cultural identity. |
| | Adopt tuakana–teina approaches to learning. |
| | Seek guidance from Pacific teachers, support staff, and parents. |
| | Be vulnerable, curious about learners and their families, and open to learning. |
| | Give others licence, in an ongoing way, to improve your use of language, pronunciation, and cultural understandings. |

| My role | My actions |
|---|---|
| Teaching | Start the day with a pure or lotu to set the scene for the day's shared activities and learning.<br><br>Teach and use greetings in Pacific languages.<br><br>Use enquiry and other methods that ensure student autonomy, with learners part of the learning decision-making processes.<br><br>Backtrack when learners are not following the teaching. |
| Celebrating | Celebrate the Language Week of each ethnicity each Pacific child has whakapapa to.<br><br>Organise regular cultural events in the learning context and with parents with themes such as food, art, dance, song, or oral traditions.<br><br>Include performances and participation with students and families.<br><br>Co-ordinate events for the community as a whole with local organisations. |
| Assessing and reporting | Communicate with parents and learners about learners' interests and wider worlds.<br><br>Negotiate and be clear with learners and parents about the nature, timing, and expectations of assessments and reporting. |
| Being an advocate for my Pacific colleagues, Pacific learners, and their families | Ensure there is a Pacific space—a room or mat in a space with Pacific artefacts and feel where activities and food can be shared—and ensure the space is honoured.<br><br>Find where there is space for students to do homework in the school and local libraries.<br><br>Organise information evenings and invite guest speakers such as Pacific educators and Pacific community leaders to strengthen connections between school and community. |

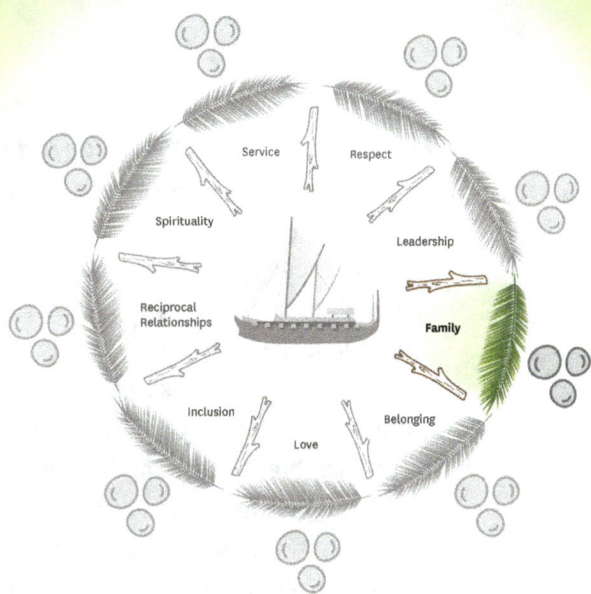

## Chapter Three

# Family

**What does family mean to Pacific people? How can learning environments strongly acknowledge and welcome the deep connections amongst family held by many Pacific children and their families?**

*Ko kaiga e taua ma pele i Tokelau*
*Ko te "INATI" e kitea ai te alowha*
*Ki ho he tino kaiga, whanau, ma tagata lautele.*

*In Tokelau our families are precious to us.*
*Through Inati we show our love by caring for each other and to show how much we value our elders, families, children, and community.*

We are very grateful to the Tokelauan Community in the Hutt Valley, Wellington, and to the community, fanau, teachers, and children of Matiti Tokelau Akoga Kamata for these opening thoughts. Their wisdom, cultural, language, and traditional knowledge are woven daily into the early childhood education curriculum with children. In this way, they are striving to ensure that Tokelauan children grow and learn the knowledge of being Tokelauan. Underpinning this action is the knowledge and *practice of Inati, a valued Tokelauan practice of families and community caring, sharing, and looking after each other. Malo ni.*

- Family means everything to many Pacific people. Consideration of family impacts on every important decision made, with many decisions jointly made by family.
- Learners whose sense of family is understood, respected, and nurtured in their learning environments are more likely to be comfortable, at ease, and learn well.
- Parents feel family is respected by learning communities when they are welcomed, respected, and involved, and when there is true partnership between the school, the family, and the learner in setting learning goals and learning experiences.
- Educators can ensure Pacific learners' sense of family is supported by knowing the names and connections of family members who are important to learners and using these understandings to inform their planning, teaching, and interactions with learners and their parents.
- Effective educators provide clear expectations and support for Pacific learners, treating Pacific learners as family.

This chapter explores the importance of family to Pacific learners. Family and family experiences are key sources of security, identity, and achievement for Pacific people (Chu et al., 2013; Si'ilata, 2014). Pacific parents expect the best education for their children and have high expectations of their children's educators (Education Review Office, 2008). Family and the communities the family is part of can provide rich and important sources of inspiration for Pacific learners. These connections can stimulate rich learner visual and oral narratives that speak to their feeling of place within society and social justice, and demonstrate the power of learning that intertwines learner, family, and community worlds (Dyck, 2021). Partnerships between learning environments and home are important for promoting learning and achievement and can benefit from opportunities for Pacific parents to have their views heard, share in their child's successes, and help their children with learning (Education Review Office, 2008; Flavell, 2017).

Many of our participants were emotional when they spoke of family, speaking with tears in their eyes. Understanding how to ensure learning environments and teaching reflect the importance of family for Pacific learners and families is vital for maximising wellbeing and achievement of Pacific learners. In this chapter, we present ideas about the value of *family* shared by experienced Pacific educators across early childhood, school, and tertiary settings.

Let's hear from our Pacific educators …

## *What does family mean to you?*

The value of family is everything. Sorry, I've started crying already. You are born into a family. For me, my mother gave birth to me. She couldn't look after me, but my grandparents did, so I didn't have an immediate Mum and Dad. Family is everything because you are born into a family, your Mum gives birth to you, but you've got your grandparents or there is a family network there that will take that responsibility to look after you if need be. It's everything because my grandparents taught me the values that they were instilling in my aunties and uncles—I was like the tenth sibling because there were nine of them. Family is important because they are the ones who nurture you. Now I have my own family, but family to me is not just them—I still think about my grandparents who brought me up in that Fijian island village setting and who have now passed away. The family there were all together, we shared everything. Nothing really belonged to anybody. If you wanted this, you had it, and you did everything for the happiness and the love for everybody.

Last week one of my uncles passed away. He was very close to my Mum, but my Mum's got Alzheimer's so she can't remember it. So, my other uncle who is here said, "Let's get together to take a moment to think about the uncle that passed." I took my Mum there because it is really important—this is how we know where we've come from. There were connections there from this uncle who passed away who was always looking after the extended family. For him, family wasn't just my children, it is my brother's children, my sister's children, my granddad's family, everyone. This is how we trace and connect back and remember. When people pass away, it's how we keep those connections going, how you keep that sense of family alive. It's very special and important to have that connection through family.

In a Pasifika way of living, it's not just the immediate parents who are involved, you've also got the grandparents, and if they're attached to church—that's practically the village that that child belongs to— so everyone who forms that village for the child has an influence and has made that child the way they are. Of course, at times when parents have emergencies, the kids are cared for by outside families or extended family, so they become parents as well.

I can give you a long lecture about family. It's everything. It's your village, that's your home, your heart—as much as you leave your nest and leave your parents, you never leave the heart that was embedded and instilled in you. Wherever you go, it doesn't matter whether you create your own family, that heart continues and continues to your next generation and so on. It's not just in your own new family, it's in the community that you're a part of, at church, in Sunday School, in choir, or whatever you do. The way you are was built from your family. Without your family you wouldn't be standing. I look at the kids in front of me at school and I go back home, and I say to my kids, "Be thankful. You have no idea of the lives of these other kids." Some come from homes where they've been uplifted in the middle of the night. We've got kids who go home and their parents are lying concussed or comatose on the front lawn from P or whatever. I tell my kids, "You're lucky you're walking into a house that belongs to you and that you've got a Mum and Dad. You're not one of those kids who are listed as a statistic under the government system."

The Pacific notion of family is a lot broader and a lot deeper than in the Western model of the nuclear two parent, two children sort of family. Family incorporates a lot of people for Pacific children. Family includes everyone, like your second and third cousin and your uncle, and it expands as the family expands. Everyone in the family's wellbeing is enhanced from knowing we have those connections. We almost go out of our way to make family connections; they're usually blood connections but may not be. Often in a family gathering, we'll be told about the connections, "Now, she's your mother's aunty, from there." Our children know who their cousins are. Close family friends are seen as family and are called aunty or uncle by the children as for blood-related aunties and uncles. Children are involved in all our family activities—they learn so much from these occasions about the family and how things are done and what is expected. These experiences tell us that we are part of this wider group, and these people know that they are part of us. It's a whole connecting with others that is very inclusive. It's broader than just, "This is where I live now." The connections are also about making links back to our home islands and communities. It is like the family claiming that you come from this island, and you are expected to make sure that you know all your island connections. It might be that you've got Manahiki connections and Palmerston connections and Tahiti connections. There's a whole sense of identity we get from knowing these family ties which feeds into our sense of belonging and inclusion. So, our sense of family is a very broad concept—that notion of hanau (family) we call it.

In my experience, when we meet with family, we make all the necessary connections about recent happenings—making sure that we know what is happening for all of the family members. For instance, my cousin passed away last week and he's my first cousin. He wanted it kept very quiet, but the telephone and the emails were all happening regardless because, for everyone, contacting others was their way of contributing to the family. He didn't want to have a big fuss made, but we wanted to contribute money to help his closer family to ensure that they didn't have to personally cover lots of costs. So, that sense of family is very strong. It's almost like we have a sense of indebtedness because we have close family connections. We owe each other and have a responsibility to make sure that everything is working well for everyone. For many Pacific people, family is tied up with other values—like your responsibility to provide service and knowing that support comes back to you when it's needed, through actions from the notion of reciprocal relationships.

Family is huge for me actually. Everything is centred around the family for me. Being the eldest in my family means there are some characteristics and responsibilities from being the eldest that I have to live by. The eldest gets to be the bossy one, but everything I do centres

> *Everything is centred around the family*

around family. Whatever happens comes back to family. I remember going for job interviews and they say, "Is there anything else you want to say?", and I always say, "My family is important, so if I have to go because of whatever family reason, I need to be given that opportunity or that time." I stress that every time. I've always felt it's important to share that so that they're aware of where I'm coming from.

Family is big for me. For my family, family is often also tied up within the community churches. It's a little different now that I'm older, I'm not so involved in church. When we were little, we used to go everywhere—our parents would take us to every little meeting, every little fundraiser. We were part of anything they were doing. A lot of my Mum's family are here in New Zealand. I have a lot of cousins—more than 60 first cousins here—and that bond is strong as we have regular get togethers. I know all my first cousins and we reach out to each other. All that sense of connection is probably nurtured through my mother and her siblings because they have always done this. We've observed them arguing then making up and they're quite open as siblings. In my Mum's family, everyone's business is everyone's business. Not all Pacific families are like that, but for us, that's what we've seen growing up. My Dad's family's a little different. They live more like a Westernised way of thinking about family, where it is your husband or wife and your children and that's it.

I would say family is probably more important than anything else. I have just been thinking about my own career and what I want to do and what is important to me, and family would probably be the most important thing to me. There is this thing that some Pacific Islanders say, and it is like "family to loyalty". It means family to the death, which means that they would choose to protect, uphold, and maintain the family above other things. For me, family is who I am. I feel so strongly about family that I actually feel like crying. When we interviewed our students on video of what success means to them, one of the really powerful things students said was that success is about making their family proud. That's very different to seeing success as something about each individual. We know that Pacific students and

> *one of the really powerful things students said was that success is about making their family proud*

Pacific staff here at school are representing their family. It's like the Māori proverb too: It's not mine alone, the success—I actually have a whole lot of people cheering me on.

To me, family is everything; it's at the core with my faith. Everything I do is for the family; family is at the forefront and the centre of everything. I didn't understand it when I was younger. My parents would lecture me and say, "You know, you carry your family's name everywhere you go and so your actions affect and come back to the family." It's almost like a way to try and keep you on the straight and narrow, so you don't go out of those boundaries and bring shame or give your family a bad reputation. But the other side is that there's strong support everywhere I go. I had a 5-year break away from family when I was overseas—and I think I could say I was a bit lost without them. I connected with people overseas that were of similar backgrounds and values, so the Kiwis, the Māori, the Samoans over there and that was my family away from family, so I still had that base.

I have my family close by, everywhere I go and any school event I have, I will always invite my family—it's not for me, it's for the students. I know that my family support my role at this school, and I had my Mum and brother bring me up to the marae at the pōwhiri when I started here. When our school held a Pacific success evening, both my parents and my brother came; they didn't need to come but they wanted to come. Also, I have brought my brother in and help drum for Polyclub and tutor the boys. So, yes, family is everything and is integral to how I do my work.

In my case, we have a really broad picture of family and within that each person can choose where they want to be, but you're often drawn on which is reminding you, particularly if you want to belong to the community, there is that sense of obligation, such as knowing that, because she is your aunty, you need to be going to see her. Last week was Cook Island language week and I went to the kaikai which was a gathering during the day before I was teaching, and the first thing my aunty said to me was, "Where have you been?" I was thinking, "Oh, I know I don't spend enough time with them," and so I said, "Yes, I know. I've been busy working, but I need to come and see you more often." My aunty saying that was her indicator that I need to have a bit more involvement there. That's just her way, but our old people are like that—they're there to remind you of the family expectations. So, my perception of family is really broad—I'm coming from a Polynesian perspective. We usually come from very large families and that makes it even broader.

I strongly uphold my cultural identity. I'm Niuean. It's not until I took on this job that I started to learn more of my Cook Island culture. My name is a Cook Island name, but I didn't associate myself as a Cook Island person—my Mum's Niuean and my Dad is Cook Island from Rarotonga. Niuean was the language that was spoken at home too and my grandmother lives with us. I feel our generation are the ones wanting to take hold of our culture and our identity and try and push that onto the following generations.

*How does the value of family play out for learners in your learning environments? How can educators respond to the Pacific value of family in their teaching and interactions?*

Teachers knowing and understanding that if something is happening to someone in the class or school, like a Samoan family or a Fijian family, that somehow, the children would all be connected in the community, they will all know each other and be involved. So, for happy occasions, sad occasions, there's a lot of people involved and there will be different roles that those people play in the occasions depending on how close they are to that family. The event will be known about in the community. What's also really neat is when teachers recognise a name or know where they live or are from, and ask, "Oh, do you know such and such?" Then the teachers will understand that it's not just one set of parents or family involved, but others will be connected. It is good if teachers make an effort to realise that it's not just Mum and Dad, there is a wider network and they can try and find those connections. For example, I've got a little one in creche, and my sister can pick him up, my brothers-in-law can pick him up—so that to me is teachers understanding family and that there will be other people as well as parents involved in the child's upbringing.

I draw on the importance of family when I work with my Tongan learners, because I really want my pupils to be happy, and I don't want to lose their sense of family. That's the angle I come from because we don't know about any other angle. When I approach the parents about something, the next day I see a lot of difference from the student. Most of our parents feel our school management already understand the importance of family to our learners. Every parent interview, I'm very honest, and the parents and children listen. I can ask a question about something not so great that has happened in a day and ask them "Why are your parents sending you to school?" and then we move on and just forget it happened. If we keep reminding the child about why they are sent to school by their family, it's going to sit inside their mind, and they will think about it. I tell them "Listen carefully, for some of you, both of your parents go to work because of your future, so do you think they pay for your school uniform for you to come and play around?" The kids didn't understand that. They didn't realise that. And I talk like that to encourage them.

### Example in practice: Asking parents' views

Respect, humility, and loyalty were pillars of how things were done in one Tongan immersion classroom we visited. Learners were asked to ask their parents what respect means to them. They came back with different views from their parents and grandparents, and all of these were displayed together in the classroom and discussed to work out together how respect would be understood and practised in their class. The same process was used for humility and loyalty, and these ideas usually came back to acting respectfully. This process involved family in school learning from the start. It set up good communication with parents, demonstrated the importance of reciprocal relationships, and helped everyone see that expectations are shared between the learners, the parents, and the educator.

In teaching, I think you can appeal to Pacific students' sense of family when things go wrong. In my role, I am often dealing with the more challenging incidents and issues. I use family in a positive way to tap into their pride in who they are and who their family is. Also, if I say to a Pacific student, "What would your Mum think about that?", or "How is your Dad going to feel when you go home or when I ring them?", that's the point where it really hits them about whatever has happened.

We really encourage using "circle work" at our school as a relationship-building and restorative practice. At any time, we can have a circle. It could be something very simple to start off with—"What's your favourite movie?"—and then go on as the year progresses to deeper things—"What's something that is really important to you?", or whatever. In the circles, they can talk about their family—they can tell us and each other about someone who is really important or special to them. These things are really useful for teachers to know as they have a better understanding of who their students are and where they come from. It is also important for everyone's sense of being within our school family and of our school's overarching and underpinning priority of everyone being part of our school family. The classroom routines like circles are a way of helping everyone feel they belong and are known. Our school values and the school family are emphasised in many ways, including in posters in every classroom. The strategies are all deliberate to help all students have that sense that they are part of something more than themselves, and that we support each other—they fit with the nurturing of family as a Pasifika value and a Māori value.

Thinking of the collective good as opposed to a Western sense of individual good, we encourage teachers to use a sense of family in their teaching practices. This can even just be encouraging students to help each other with work, "You know, you are good at that so can you help your neighbour there?" One of our teachers doing their teaching inquiry is focusing on consistently using that approach as a culturally responsive way of working with her students. She met quite a bit of resistance when she started saying, "Right, you are finished? Then you are going to go and help so and so", but now students are used to it and it is happening all of the time.

Within the language nest or the early childhood setting, school, or tertiary classroom, we as Pacific educators can bring a lot of our sense of family into the space. We can share which groups we're a part of and that now we're part of your family as well. Although we're not connected by blood relationship, we see ourselves as part of your group as much as we can be. We have to be strongly attuned to the families of our learners and know what being part of their families entails for our learners. We need to be open and alert to possibilities of how we nurture the sense of family in these settings even more strongly. We do this by knowing the cultural practices of the groups the children's families are part of. Knowing these things can be hugely advantageous to us as teachers, as we are better placed to make suitable decisions about the learning experiences we offer and the ways we interact with each learner. However, sadly, I don't think that type of knowledge is recognised as an important part of developing new teachers or teacher professional development yet. It should be.

When I teach, I always use my family as my examples. A lot of the stories I share to make teaching points involve my family. This also enables my learners to be comfortable to do the same—when I ask them to share ideas, they are more likely to share examples from within their family. I also offer a coffee time so they can come for a coffee and a chat, not only about the course but other things they may have questions about for their futures as well. Even though I've got 200 students in that class, I really want to be intimate in terms of knowing them and getting involved. I want them to understand that my relationship with them is not only about the course—I also have a level of care for them—I don't do too much, but it's enough to give them that sense, "I'm here if you need it."

The students who are connected to me in some family way know what I'm like. My cousins or cousins' children are the ones here now. If they miss a class, I'll say, "I didn't see you in class today." I tend to do that a lot with the Pacific students, even if I don't know them. I'll just mention to them, "I haven't seen you in class", treating them as I treat the students in my family. Last year I would stop at the gym to collect a couple of them that didn't look like they were going to stop and come to class and just take them through to class with me. That's that whole sense of treating them as family, showing them, "Come on, we can do this" to support them.

I give strong encouragement through my emails to students as well. For instance, when we're halfway through the course, we send out a reminder of what they need to do to pass the course, to tell them and to show our expectations of them. Then I'll get emails, saying, "Oh, I didn't know, and I had to do chores." Then, the first thing I'll say is, "Oh, I really appreciate your email", to acknowledge that they've taken this step, even though

I'm thinking, "Where have you been for 6 weeks and why didn't you know this?" But I will always make sure that send a response back that shows I really appreciate them making the effort to contact me. These are things that all our lecturers and educators, Pacific and non-Pacific, can be doing to treat our students as family.

*How can non-Pacific educators develop the knowledge and understandings needed to respond to the importance of family to Pacific learners and their families?*

Meeting with families is a privilege because it really gives you the bigger picture for each learner. We encourage our teachers to be in touch with families, to be in communication with home, to enable parents to be a part of the learning journey, inviting them to be a part of it. We also use academic conferencing where we invite the family in, and we have got the pōwhiri and celebrations. There are more opportunities to invite parents in here than at some other schools. The hall was jam packed at the Pacific Success evening which tells you a lot—the whole family is there to celebrate success. We could do even more to bring families in. Most of our teachers here are good at communicating with home and informing them of what is going on with their child at school. It's case by case but I have seen it happening a lot.

In our initial teacher education programme, we talk about Pacific families and communities, but we only have time to do this quite broadly and it's certainly not going to be as deeply understood for many of our student teachers as for those who have lived this way, building up this knowledge over many years and experiences. I think some student teachers think that the cultural aspect of the programme is just one thing that they can tick off as done, without realising how much depth exists and is needed for their understanding. Those fortunate enough to be based in a language nest for their practicum see how family can be foregrounded in children's learning. It gives them an insight into how things happen within a culturally based community in comparison to what may be done in English-medium contexts. Like in these settings, entire teaching teams need to be attuned to Pacific values and language for student teachers to have very useful experiences and learning about working with Pacific learners.

### What might be done differently by teachers in Pacific-based and non-Pacific-based learning environments, in terms of family?

Often in a language nest, the teachers are also parents and they have their mokopuna and children there so these places are already like broad family units. They run in a very family village-type way and a lot are connected to the church. They'll have a management group which is like the matai, the hierarchy, and then they'll have the teachers. They have a family connection. When you arrive, there's a feeling of walking into a village—all of the artefacts, the language, the protocols, and that wider sense of family are there. There are the mats and the shells and music playing. All these things impact on children's identity, their language, the environment, and their experience of the Pacific values—how they can be lived, felt, experienced, demonstrated, and nurtured. Student teachers may not experience that feeling in other centres unless they're in a mainstream early childhood centre where the majority of the children are Pacific.

The Pacific students who come to our university all know each other or have a sense of each other based on their own community. If something is going on in the community, they would all kind of talk about it. In terms of tertiary, if a tutor or lecturer hears of something that's going on in the Samoan community or Fijian community, like that someone has passed away or something like that, the lecturer could take the initiative to talk with the student about any deadlines and work out with them a realistic time frame to get the work in. Ideally, the lecturer should be proactive rather than wait for the student to make a request. That's important for Pacific learners, because there is a sense in tertiary that students are adults and they should speak and come forward and know what they want. However, I experienced this in my first attempt at university and I wasn't sure if I could do that back then. There's a tension of "I should be an adult and I should meet this

> *if a tutor or lecturer hears of something that's going on in the Samoan community or Fijian community, like that someone has passed away or something like that, the lecturer could take the initiative to talk with the student about any deadlines and work out with them a realistic time frame to get the work in.*

deadline", but "I also have my obligations to my family". That's a downfall for a lot of tertiary students when they come in—understanding that expectation that, "I'm an adult now, I've got time frames that I have to meet, but that I may not meet once something happens in my family or community." Family then takes priority. As a Pacific person, it's almost like you've got no flexibility with the university life. I think it would be great in this situation if a lecturer or a tutor acknowledged what is happening and asked, "How long do you need and when can we re-set this time frame for this particular project?"

Many of the universities are trying hard to increase their numbers of Pacific students, get bums on seats, but the retention team then has the job of trying to keep them here—which is just as important as bringing them in, or more so because they're in and they've paid and the university has a responsibility to change the way they do things to make university a positive and, even better, a great experience for Pacific learners. What I learnt at my second attempt at university is that you have just got to ask, and to explain your situation and see what happens—and it's great, the lecturers are awesome, but I wouldn't know that if I hadn't sent off that first email. For many of our Pacific tertiary students, they're still that quiet Pacific person who is probably still doubting the fact that they made it this far—so there is often a bit of self-doubt until maybe a year and a half into tertiary study, because then they know they've come half way.

In summary, attending to the value of family means caring for each other and valuing elders, children, and community. Having a deep and shared sense of the importance of family from birth throughout life is normal for many Pacific people, with family central to Pacific people's lives, thinking, and decision making. Valuing family means knowing your connections with others, meeting expectations and responsibilities, and realising how your actions impact on your family members. Family is a source of support, inspiration, and cultural identity. For many Pacific people, family is more important than anything else.

**Discussion questions**

Tahi   *What understandings and practices are necessary for creating learning environments that deeply value family?*

Lua   *How can educators share about their own families and learn about the families of their learners?*

Tolu   *What can educators do to create learning environments where families are acknowledged, valued, and involved?*

**Ideas for extra reading**

**Partners in learning: Parents' voices**
Education Review Office (2008)

This report shares Pacific parents' expectations and recommendations around schools providing their children with a good education and excellent use of English. Parents saw their homes as foundational to learning and maintaining their mother tongue. Pacific parents experienced schools expecting their support in running cultural groups and supporting their children's homework. They appreciated newsletters being translated into their first language, being a part of the board, and face-to-face communication, which made them feel involved and valued. Language barriers affected the engagement of some Pacific parents.

**See me, know me, believe in me: Reimagining Pasifika student success as Pasifika in visual arts**
Dyck (2021)

The importance of family and how this can be acknowledged and family experiences drawn from learning experiences are clear in this, article which describes visual arts as providing a safe space for learners to draw from their identities and express their voices and stories. Examples of learners' artwork and notions of success and presented.

**Listening to and learning from Pacific families**
Flavell (2017)

Taking time to listen and build relationships, important for meaningful discussions between parents, teachers, and student participation are discussed in this article. The article emphasises teachers listening to Pacific families—as to be heard is to feel valued.

**Pasifika students: Teachers and parents voice their perceptions of what provides supports and barriers to Pasifika students' achievement in literacy and learning**
Fletcher, Parkhill, Fa'afoi, Taleni, & O'Regan (2009)

Supports and challenges to Year 5 to Year 9 Pacific learner literacy achievement are discussed in this article. Differences in the way families live in their home island and in New Zealand are proposed as contributing to some Pacific learners having less learning support in the New Zealand context than in their home island. Ways to improve Pacific learner literacy and draw from their cultural knowledge and language identities are presented.

## References

Chu, C., Abella, I., & Paurini, S. (2013). *Educational practices that benefit Pacific learners in tertiary education*. Ako Aotearoa. https://ako.ac.nz/assets/Knowledge-centre/NPF-10-001A-Pasifika-Learners-and-Success-in-Tertiary-Education/RESEARCH-REPORT-Educational-Practices-that-Benefit-Pacific-Learners-in-Tertiary-Education.pdf

Dyck, D. (2021). See me, know me, believe in me: Reimagining Pasifika student success as Pasifika in visual arts. *Set: Research Information for Teachers*, (2), 4–17. : https://doi.org/10.18296/set.0198

Education Review Office. (2008). *Partners in learning: Parents' voices*. Author. https://ero.govt.nz/sites/default/files/2021-05/Partners-in-Learning-Parents-Voices-Sep08.pdf

Flavell, M. (2017). Listening to and learning from Pacific families. *Set: Research Information for Teachers*, (2), 42–48. doi: https://doi.org/10.18296/set.0074

Fletcher, J., Parkhill, F., Fa'afoi, A., & O'Regan, B. (2009). Pasifika students, teachers and parents voice their perceptions of what provides supports and barriers to Pasifika students' achievement in literacy and learning. *Teaching and Teacher Education, 25*(1), 24–33. https://doi.org/10.1016/j.tate.2008.06.002

Si'ilata, R. (2014). *Va'a Tele: Pasifika learners riding the success wave on linguistically and culturally responsive pedagogies*. Doctoral thesis, The University of Auckland. http://hdl.handle.net/2292/23402

# Educator practice—Demonstrating and nurturing family

| My role | My actions |
|---|---|
| **Interacting with learners** | Treat learners as family. |
| | Learn about my learners using learners, parents, and family as sources. |
| | Encourage learners to meet expectations and strive to achieve learning goals. |
| | Nurture positive educator-learner relationships in all interactions and teaching. |
| | Ask learners to prepare a family tree/web to share at the beginning of the year, so that the educator can know about their extended family and people special to them who may be involved in their learning. |
| | Share some aspects of your own family to help nurture relationships. |
| **Interacting with parents and families** | Involve and develop relationships with families in enrolment processes, welcomes, and many events. |
| | Include family members, as chosen by families, in conversations and academic conferencing, connecting to their cultural understandings. |
| | Work to ensure feelings of connectedness between families and the learning environment. |
| | Knowing about families and the importance of family for learners can provide a powerful sense of connection for educators. |
| **Planning** | Be aware that Pacific families can be extensive, multigenerational, and connected. |
| | Plan regular circle times or class discussions revolving around family. |
| | Start with general relatable topics and move into discussion around special family members admired by learners. |
| | Know the cultural practices of your learners. |
| | Understand that family obligations may need to take priority for learners. |
| **Teaching** | Use examples from your own family and groups you are part of in your teaching so learners understand who you are and so that dialogue and consideration of family are encouraged. |
| | Encourage learners to help each other. |
| **Celebrating** | Incorporate academic conferencing in events and ceremonies. |
| | Set up regular Pacific Success evenings. |
| **Assessing and reporting** | Using understanding of relevant cultural protocols, warmly invite family for discussions about learning, teaching, assessment, and reporting. |

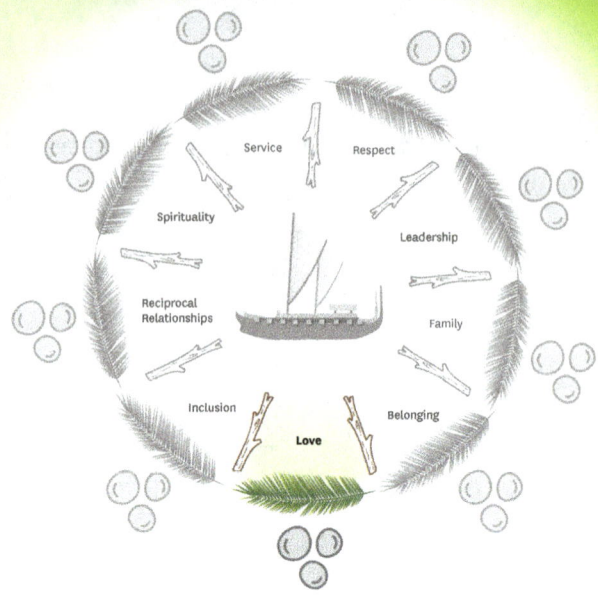

Chapter Four

# Love

**What does love mean to Pacific people? How can learning environments treasure the Pacific value of love?**

*E teianei, te vai nei te akarongo, te manakonako, e te aroa, e toru ra; ko tei maata ra i taua toru nei, ko te aroa īa.*
*1 Korinetia 13:13*

*Meanwhile these three remain: faith, hope, and love; and the greatest of these is love.*
*1 Corinthians 13:13*

*We warmly thank the teachers at Te Punanga o Te Reo Kuki Airani in Wellington, the first Pacific language nest to be set up in New Zealand, for sharing this perspective on love. All were involved in deciding the thoughts about love to share, remembering all their Mamas and Papas who have passed who recited the verse regularly. All teachers at Te Punanga o Te Reo Kuki Airani are of Cook Island ethnicity and their programme is bilingual. The language nest's philosophy focuses on promoting Cook Island values, language, and culture to children in their care to ensure these are imparted, cherished, enjoyed, and preserved. Meitaki ma'ata.*

- Love for one another as family is practised and expected by many Pacific people's way of thinking.
- Having a deep sense of love for others and giving from the heart are part of what it means to be a Pacific person.
- Showing love for others governs actions and reactions of Pacific people.
- Feeling love for our learners and for advancing their learning can help lead to developing the strong positive educator–learner relationships necessary to many Pacific learners for maximising achievement and wellbeing.

In this chapter, we focus on how love, giving, and working from the heart are understood and exemplified by experienced Pacific heritage educators across early childhood, school, and tertiary settings. Love, alofa, 'ofa, shown in how we interact and give to others, is an important and accepted way of living and being for many Pacific people. Showing your heart, which can be seen as where intellect, emotion, and spirit converge, is important for being true to yourself, bringing your true self to teaching and learning tasks and building rapport (Koerner, 2020). Love is shown to family, one's village, community, area, and country (Va'a, 2009) and is key to service being carried out suitably (Tagoilelagi-Leota, 2017).

Care for others, essential for effective educator–learner relationships, stems from love. Effective teaching involves educators demonstrating passion for what they are teaching and care for learners and is emotional and embodied as well as cognitive (Anderson et al., 2020). Learners benefit greatly from teachers passionate about teaching and about learners, teachers who get to the heart, beauty, and power of the learning content and act as partners in learning inspiring learners to search for knowledge and insight (Thomas, 2007). Such teaching helps shape learners' attitudes to learning and aspirations.

Let's hear from our Pacific educators ...

*What does the value of love mean to you?*

Some people might refer to love as aroha or alofa. The word "love" seems quite weird actually—it's not often we say the word. Well, every time I see one of my little nieces and nephews, I say "I love you", but when you actually talk about the word love, it sounds strange to discuss. It feels better to say aroha or alofa; it flows better and takes that whole romantic interpretation of love out of it.

Love is what drives my decision making in my family. I'm in a bit of a conundrum if I look back in my own family—my husband and I are from different islands of Fiji and his take on our children is completely different to mine. He's more the disciplinarian, and he sometimes doesn't get why I pause and want to talk about it and think about it myself in my head before reacting. So I can see that how I was brought up is very different to how my daughter's being brought up, but she's Year 10, her reports have been amazing, she is driven, she wants to learn, we don't need to tell her what to do, she's a good learner. What I ask my husband a lot is about who we are bringing up our children for—for ourselves, so that they listen to us, or are we bringing them up to be ready for the world when they go out into it? Because what I found when I went out into the world is, "I know what my values are and my respect for my culture"; however, the world is a bit different, so we need to find a way to meet in the middle. I realised when I went overseas that doing things differently doesn't mean I'm disrespecting my Fijian identity—it's just what I need to do to be in this environment. It doesn't make me less Fijian; it just means that I have more ability to offer in that environment. What I'm trying to instil in my children is a foundation from where they can branch out.

The whole idea of the value of love or aroha or alofa is wide. It connects with bigger ideas like care, with that whole idea of if you do alofa to this young person, when you do this, you'll be caring for them. It's more than just giving a hug—it's actually trying to understand where they're coming from and when they leave, you say, "See you later, see you next year."

Aroha is not just for here or there, it's more that we're all in this page together which can only be improved by better understanding of where people are coming from and what expectations might be that might be different from our own.

### How is love experienced by Pacific people outside of education?

For us in our community, and especially in our families, love for us is getting told off—they used to say, "That's love, that's family love, you're getting told off." To our island parents, that's part of showing their love to their young kids. It's about teaching. I think some physical sort of punishment still goes on, along with saying, "I do this because I love you." There are other ways of giving these messages now, and we've moved on from that type of way of showing love.

### Is love giving?

Yes, to me, aroha has more of a sense of a gifting than the word love. If you have that love for others, that's what triggers service and respect in the way you act. You give everything away, "I love you, so here have this. What can I do for you?" Love is what motivates us to make sure that everyone is well looked after, is cared for, and that's showing love—it's being a good host, making sure that everyone is well, all is well in the world, that's how you demonstrate love. I don't think it's just a Pacific action, I think many people think like that, but we demonstrate it in the way that we give things, like making sure that we have plenty of food and so, when people come, they feel as if you're a good host; that's showing love. When you've got a function, you take as much food as you can and when there's a funeral, you give as much money as you can; that's showing that we really want to show our love in this way. So, love is in our actions, in what we do, what we can provide.

> *love is in our actions, in what we do, what we can provide.*

### How is love present in your teaching?

Love is embedded in how I think. For example, actions speak louder than words, and that really goes with love. What you do, how you show love is more important than just saying, "I love you." Love is helping, it's being there for somebody, caring but also being open to looking around to seeing what there is that you can do to help. Love is getting joy out of helping somebody because that's how you show your love—whether it is in or outside a learning setting. Children can read you. People can read you, so be authentic because children are not silly. They can read you. Teachers giving an explanation about why they do certain things in a classroom would give more understanding for children and empathy than not explaining. Showing love is always having time for that person. It's trying to understand why they do things from their perspective and then trying to meet them in the middle of what you're trying to explain or get them to do. If there's a need to discipline or manage behaviour, do it in a loving way where they're not scared, but they know where the line is and can still express themselves.

There's no "love" in my courses at all. I just say get on with it. However, I do know that the students come to see me if they've got concerns, or needs, or extensions and I don't think that they would do that unless they felt comfortable to do so and that their request would be met with a loving approach. I try in the way I set up feelings of belonging and inclusion in my classes, which shows students that I am prepared to listen to them and I see them as individuals who have got things happening in their lives. One of the key things with my biggest course is having great tutors who understand my priority that they show understanding about where the students are coming from. For example, one of my tutors was really struggling with a group of Pacific students who were giving her a hard time. She had decided to respond by marking their work hard and giving no extensions. So, we had a big talk and I said to her, "Actually a big part of dealing with this situation is your heart—the heart that goes in to talking with and listening to your students. Being part of being a good tutor is that you've got to have the heart for all students, including those who are pains up the bum, excuse my lingo. Then you know they will come to you because they know that you've shown them that heart, which is that aroha, because they wouldn't come to us if they don't feel this."

We have had students who come to us from our other 100-level courses who are not our students but they're good friends with people who are, and they come because they are confident that we are good people to connect with. When we get the emails asking for an extension, we have an informal conversation with them and hear where they're coming from and discuss how can we work on this together. I've always said to my tutors, "You always take each one seriously no matter what." We let the learners know that we are there for them no matter what. I think that shows what aroha's all about. I encourage the learners to know in the emails and in our lectures that the tutors are here for them—they're not here because they get big money for it.

> *We let the learners know that we are there for them no matter what.*

Our institution has good support now for Pacific learners. When I get a call from one of the student support team, I listen, but I also try to make contact back to the student to let them know I've had this conversation and know where they're coming from and I'd really like for us to have a talk. It's like the support team is part of the institution's loving face.

For me, love is never giving up on students, always assuming the best, and always working and never giving up. You've entered into that relationship and so you care enough about that person that you wouldn't want to give up, why would you give up? A lot goes on here with people reaching out to students to support them.

These days there are lots of stresses on many of our Pacific families and their children are more vulnerable because they have more time without their parents around. So, love extends to care for their learners in the wider sense—being aware of all of the kinds of things that might happen and the risks and dangers, and being alert and showing that care for the wider person through their actions.

Love is being caring and open and understanding of all our tamariki who come into our centre, making sure everyone has that warm feeling when they come in and feels invited as they come in. Love is also being there for the tamariki if they need help, being reliable. Love in action is hugs and a kiss on the cheek which we give to tamariki in our Pacific centres. That affection is really important culturally, something we promote in the way we work with our children. Children need that particularly as we're nurturing them, not only in their physical wellbeing but their whole holistic development.

Showing love in teaching comes back to knowing each individual child and the family that they come from and how they live their lives in their wider worlds, so that I can replicate some of that in this place. It's also about showing caring and concern and taking time and making the extra effort for each child, even if they're students that you haven't immediately formed a connection with. I'm showing love by taking time and getting to know these kids, what makes them tick, what is it about this place that works or doesn't work for them, how can we change it so that they are each fostering a love of being in this place as well.

Love is demonstrated in the way that I look after my family and how I work with other people, the way I teach my students, how I work with them, showing care and concern. They see that I look out for them, I'm here for them. It comes through in my teaching and how I look after the students that I teach—they are important and we're all here together. I'm you, I'm part of the group. Power roles don't work for me. I'm there right beside others and for me it's about us all facing the same direction. I want them to feel enthused and take the ideas and carry them through in their practice as well. That comes from a place of love. It's putting everyone else before you.

### How is love for your learners similar to love for your own children?

Love for me as a Pasifika and Niuean teacher is something that comes naturally, just as for a mother. You have that passion, that love within your heart, which is why you're teaching, because you're passionate about the job that you do. Love naturally comes with that, and with love comes your cultural values, your beliefs. You nurture these children with your spirituality as well, all those feelings come in. It's who you are as a person to embody this love. It's how we were raised. We incorporate all those things into the way we see these children. We don't just see them as children coming into the centre. We see them as our own children who their parents trust you to take care of for 8 hours a day, so we build a relationship with them, we bring with us all the teaching that we were brought up with.

Love is important. That's where all the comfort comes from, the caring, the trust. That's how we build the relationship with the children that we look after. If we don't have these values, it's pointless being here. If we have these natural instincts, especially as a mother—we have our own children and we show them love, we show them kindness, so these are things we also bring to our workplace—particularly in early childhood, because we are also doing a lot of the caregiving and the nurturing and it goes hand in hand, doesn't it.

> *If we don't have these values, it's pointless being here.*

For me, love is making sure everyone is happy. So, I just say it straight to parents, "Are you happy? If you're not, I'll change things." The heart inside me wants my kids to be happy—honestly, I call all my students my kids. I use the word "kids" because inside I have a feeling for each one exactly the same as for my own children. If the teachers are not like that, the kids won't listen. They feel it. If you talk and teach with love, they feel it. If you talk from anger or hate, that makes things worse. If you just give instructions, like, "Write this down", what is that?

Our learners' parents need to see our love just as the children do. We have to make sure to show them our passion—that we love our teaching and love to teach their children and that we love their children. Every child who comes to our centre, we always treat them the same—it doesn't matter who they are, we treat them the same. Having good and honest communication with the parents is part of me showing my love for their children. The concept of aroha is more than love. There's something else involved—like belonging and spirituality, for example.

### Is love linked to cultural identity?

For me, love includes honouring my culture and feeling how lucky I am to be part of the Pacific and to be Cook Island Māori and Tahitian. Understanding the importance of love is how I was raised. Mum always drummed into us to never forget who we are, to be proud and connect to others who are also Cook Island Māori. I raise my children with the belief that they're so lucky that we are who we are, despite all of the challenges and the difficulties that we sometimes encounter. This love of my background comes from a sense of pride that my ancestors were able to live on this place which is right on the sea and move across the ocean. They were strong, capable people living close to nature who understood that ways, practices, rituals, and rights were there for a reason.

To act on my love for the learners I might have to make huge changes. I want each one to build that love of learning and education and ideas. So, I'm going to have to be creative in how I plan and teach and work around any policies or systems that might be counterproductive for my learners. It might be that every morning I stand at the door and welcome the learners each in their own language, ask them a little question, and make a mental note of their answers so I can make my teaching more relevant and inclusive of everyone. That can help me help them make connections to the learning and bring in some suitable cultural ways of teaching and learning, like tuakana–teina, ako, talanoa. We can decide to have a talanoa, get rid of all of the desks and put our mats down on the floor, like back home, back in the village. Using these strategies is exciting not only for the children who need to be supported in their cultural learning, but also for other children. Knowing about my learners helps me to be creative and honour what each of our students brings into the class, to help give them agency and empowerment. They can be a central part of my planning when I know about them. When I'm really showing love and concern and a real desire for them to do well in this place, I'm using teaching strategies that will work very well for them, motivate and empower them—that for me is what love should be about in teaching. Being inspiring and being inspired is so important and we need to cling to these ideas rather than to get bogged down in lots of the other stuff of teaching.

Love for cultural identity of who we are is shown in the way our language, practices, and artefacts are present in the learning environment. It's things like that that we look for, for connections to who we are, as symbols of who we are. For parents, when they move to Aotearoa, it wasn't their choice to give away everything from their lives outside New Zealand. They didn't want to give away their language and their culture and their identities. That's a huge sacrifice and compromise to make for education, because getting a good education for our kids and to get a good job were the big things bringing many Pacific people here. Sadly, many haven't really achieved the good job that well and the education hasn't been as good as it should be for many Pacific children because the school system and teachers haven't catered well enough for Pacific learners—but we can learn and we can make changes and that's what research and reading and thinking allow us to do.

> **Example in practice: Community involvement**
>
> On a day we were visiting one school, time was given in the day for practices for Pacific community performances to celebrate the new school hall. Each group in each practice room was managed and taught by their own Pacific parents and community members. We glimpsed the Tongan community and children working formally, the Niuean children dancing mid-performance, and a Samoan practice in another space and so on.
>
> Love for each other and the school was clear—everyone was working hard to do their best for celebrating the new building. Other Pacific values evident included respect for the knowledge and skills of community, reciprocal relationships, and spirituality. Through this work, dialogue about other matters can arise because relationships, respect, and trust have been nourished. Doors were open to parents and students experienced the school valuing cultural knowledge and skills. We saw happy children, secure in their cultural identity, enjoying being themselves and learning.

### *Do you think that some pedagogies might help with demonstrating and sharing love than others?*

Absolutely, totally. When I went to visit a student teacher, she said her pukumahi, her Māori mentor, said the best way to learn was by singing waiata. I told her that that's how I learnt to do our karakia for our food as well. I said sometimes they ask me to deliver a karakia for food and I'm so used to singing it with my children, I've got to think, "No, don't sing", and I just say it but singing lightens things up and connects us. It connects everyone in the room in different ways and that's a way of bringing us together because it's a spark that we share in this space and can show love. Many Pacific people love singing, so if there's going to be something in the classroom that's got singing in it, I am going to be right there, and I love doing it with other people. The same with dance. I can see the joy on people's faces when they're dancing and that's the perfect time for us to be feeling connected and that sense of love for the things that we're doing together. It's all teaching and learning. People who have these strengths are also able to shine.

Knowing my learners and their strengths well helps me to cater for all of the culturally responsive ways that connect our students with their learning and helps me know that I'm doing a holistic job in my teaching. They help broaden the cognitive focus, develop relationships, and incorporate a spiritual dimension. The emotional engagement and social learning come together with all that and then I know I'm doing a lot richer job, I'm bringing everyone in, and I can tell by their faces that they love being here.

An important feeling for some Pacific students is that shared excitement in experiencing singing or dancing together. It helps them engage with learning and, sadly, so much of school learning is not like that—but it could be. I think having the sense of doing something really well, all in time, all together, with a common purpose has got to help develop the sense of love for what we're doing.

Sometimes we can get a little bit traditional in our approach to work within systems or processes. We need to feel we are not constrained, but empowered to know what possibilities there are for using ideas from our upbringing to make sure that they come through in my teaching—drawing from the privileges I had to experience great ways of learning through love in my upbringing.

Aroha and education have to be seen together otherwise the children who are failing will also have a sense of not being connected to others and education. We need to make sure we bring everyone through, so we need to use pedagogies that have been a bit forgotten and bring them back into the classroom, right across into tertiary and not letting education be a dull, boring, horrible place to be. Education has to have a life.

*So, thinking about parents of our Pacific children, how can educational institutions demonstrate this value of love with the parent community?*

Yes, that can be a hard group to work with. Generally, their experiences of education have not been particularly good and so they wouldn't see education and love together. As with everything else, making time to connect with them and finding out about them and really honouring who they are as parents is important for demonstrating love. It's about building a really good solid relationship with them so that they feel safe to share. They have aspirations like everyone else, but their aspirations aren't as easy to attain. We need to find out what they want and have their voices present and felt in the way we run our institutions. We need to make sure that they are on our Board of Trustees and they want to be there, not that they've just been pulled in as the school needs a Pacific person, or we might set up a little talanoa group of Pacific parents who might then feed into the Board of Trustees as they feel more comfortable in sharing from that process.

In summary, in interactions with learners, their families and the wider learning community, and in teaching, attending to the value of love can mean endeavouring to ensure that love, faith, and hope are seen in and felt by actions and words. Love drives decision making and is shown in acts of giving and sharing. Love involves honouring cultures and individuals and ensuring everyone can be true to themselves in the learning environment. Being open, caring, and having and being clear about expectations show love and respect for others.

## Discussion questions

Tai   *What understandings and practices are necessary for creating learning environments that demonstrate and nurture alofa?*

Rua   *How can educators learn about their learners and use this knowledge in caring ways in their planning and teaching?*

Tolu   *How can educators create learning environments where learners feel loved and cared for?*

## Ideas for extra reading

**Good teaching as care in higher education**
Anderson, Rabello, Wass, Golding, Rangi, and Eteuati (2020)

This article highlights the role of care and culture in teaching and learning communication and the significance for multicultural (including Pacific) learners of tertiary educators caring about their learners as individuals. Study participants said effective educators are passionate about their discipline and care about their teaching and their learners—which can be conveyed through the educator's attentiveness and their understanding of their learners' background, wellbeing, and commitments.

**Samoan custom and human rights: An Indigenous view**
Va'a (2009)

This article discusses human rights and their connection to Samoan customs and life. Core values and beliefs discussed include alofa (love) of one's family, village, and nation. How values support one's cultural identity, cultural rights, and social advocacy are outlined.

**'Tu'utu'u le upega i le loloto—Cast the net into deeper waters': Using research and practice to rethink mathematics pedagogy: Let's dance!**
Taeao & Averill (2020)

Ways of incorporating Pacific dance into curriculum planning and teaching to create opportunities for sharing and joy in learning are discussed in this article.

## References

Anderson, V., Rabello, R., Wass, R., Golding, C., Rangi, A., Eteuati, E., ... & Waller, A. (2020). Good teaching as care in higher education. *Higher Education, 79*(1), 1–19. https://doi.org/10.1007/s10734-019-00392-6

Koerner, M. (2020). At the heart of a teacher: Schooling in a pandemic. *Journal of Interdisciplinary Studies in Education, 9*(1), 172–174. : https://doi.org/10.32674/jise.v9i1.2371

Taeao, S., & Averill, R. (2020). 'Tu'utu'u le upega i le loloto—Cast the net into deeper waters': Using research and practice to rethink mathematics pedagogy: Let's dance! *Set: Research Information for Teachers*, (1), 49–57. https://doi.org/10.18296/set.0161

Tagoilelagi-Leota, F. (2017). *Soso'o le fau I le fau: Exploring what factors contribute to Samoan children's cultural and language security from the Aoga Amata to Samoan primary bilingual classrooms in Aotearoa/New Zealand.* PhD thesis, Auckland University of Technology. https://orapp.aut.ac.nz/bitstream/handle/10292/11022/TagoilelagiLeotaF.pdf?sequence=4

Thomas, J. (2007). Teaching with passion. *The Education Digest, 73*(3), 63–65.

Va'a, U. L. F. (2009). Samoan custom and human rights: An Indigenous view. *Victoria University of Wellington Law Review, 40*(1), 237–240. https://ojs.victoria.ac.nz/vuwlr/article/view/5388

# Educator practice—Demonstrating and nurturing love/alofa/aroha

| My role | My actions |
| --- | --- |
| Interacting with learners | Forge and nurture strong positive academic relationships with my learners. |
| | Talk with and listen to learners about their needs and respond in practice. |
| | Show passion for curriculum, teaching, and helping learners succeed. |
| | Be inclusive and demonstrate that each learner and their needs are important. |
| | Show learners their educator loves their work and won't give up on them. |
| | Discuss love, alofa, aroha and what these mean to families and learners. How do they show love to their siblings, parents, community? |
| | Share with learners that educators show love by helping learners learn and wanting what is best for them. |
| Interacting with parents and families | Ensure Pacific voices are clear in decision making. |
| | Get to know families and develop mutual trust. |
| | Ensure parents and families are comfortable with you and the learning environment. |
| | Encourage parents to become involved with the learning setting. |
| | Consider ways to show love for your job and learners in your communications with parents. |
| Planning | Learn and use greetings in learners' languages. |
| | Greet learners individually. |
| | Ask learners questions and use their answers to guide planning, acknowledging their ideas. |
| Teaching | Use Pacific cultural ways of learning and discussing such as talanoa or using mats as places for discussion. |
| | Use dance and song to instil joy and assist learning. |
| | Use cultural artefacts and Pacific languages. |
| Celebrating | Celebrate every success with learners and with families. |

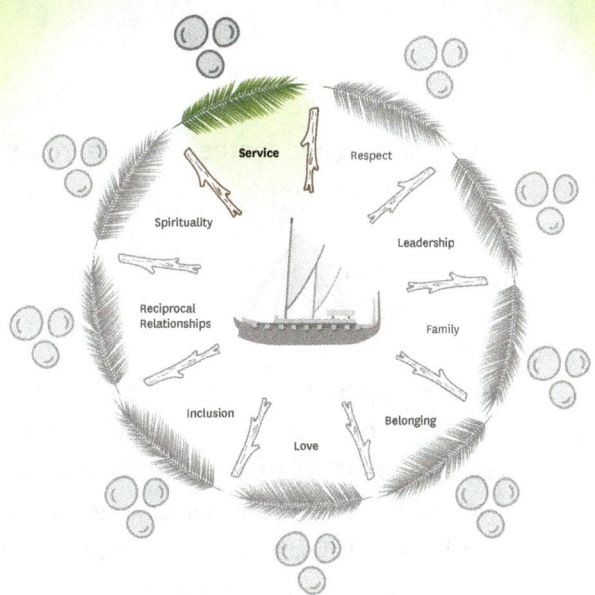

Chapter Five

# Service

**What does service mean to Pacific people? How can learning environments strongly demonstrate and nurture Pacific perspectives of service?**

> *Tautua nei mo se manuia o a Taeao*
> Serve with love, diligence, and prudence,
> for a brighter tomorrow

*We are very grateful to Malo Sepuloni for the opening thoughts for this chapter. Malo has been teaching for 26 years and is currently the team leader for the Samoan Bilingual Learning Pathway, Year 1– Year 8, at Mangere East School. Malo hails from the villages of Saanapu, Satapuala, and Magiagi and resides in Papatoetoe Auckland with her family. Fa'afetai tele lava.*

- Noticing how to be helpful and selflessly providing service to others is part of what it means to be a Pacific person and part of a Pacific family and community.
- Everyone has skills, knowledge, and effort they can provide.

- Serving one another within learning communities to ensure everyone is making learning progress can be a catalyst for learning and academic achievement.
- Learning institutions can do more to serve their Pacific learners and families.

In this chapter we focus on how giving service is an expected part of being a Pacific community member from a very young age. Service links strongly with leadership and other values such as respect and reciprocal relationships. We consider how service responsibilities and school and work commitments can be in conflict for Pacific people and ways educators can demonstrate understanding and support.

Giving service—putting others before oneself without seeking personal gain (Fairburn-Dunlop, 2010; Surtees et al., 2021; Va'a, 2009)—is fundamentally important to Pacific people, guides social actions (Surtees et al., 2021), and can help and hinder learning and achievement (Theodore et al., 2018). Many Pacific learners and their families carry out substantial service roles outside their learning environments (Fa'avae, 2017; Rimoni, 2016). Pacific elders and parents expect everyone to be of service to others (Anae, 1997). Educators can develop understanding of how Pacific students develop their service to others by recognising how Pacific students work together in cultural activities to learn about, understand, and carry out their obligations and responsibilities (Fa'avae, 2017).

Let's hear from our Pacific educators …

## *What does service mean to you?*

Service for me is very important. There is a Samoan proverb that says the pathway to leadership is through service, so service is a really big value for Samoans especially, because of that proverb. A successful person is seen as somebody who serves their community and serves others and service ties in well with leadership. If you are in a leadership role, service to the community is expected of you. It is really important to serve others. Service also ties in well with our Christian values—being of service to others like Jesus was.

Service encompasses the whole obligation to your family and to your community and to your culture that underpins everything. You don't have the option to opt out. You must respond to others' needs or requests even if it is inconvenient or you have short notice.

Service comes before anything else. It's really difficult for our Pacific students sometimes when they've got obligations—other things like schoolwork and everything else comes second to their service. Our education system doesn't see it that way, and it's hugely disadvantaging that often we don't make allowances, or we don't know we need to. We still have a system where assignments need to be handed in on a certain date and meet a certain standard, even though we don't realise that the student might have been up until midnight nursing a sick mother. My mother was a bad asthmatic; I'd have to get up in the middle of the night and massage her back because that was the only way she could breathe, and then go to school the next day. I'm sure others have far more taxing duties than that but because you want to belong to your community, you have to give back—it's that service, and if you don't give, then you don't get back and you become alienated from your community.

> *Service encompasses the whole obligation to your family and to your community and to your culture that underpins everything. You don't have the option to opt out.*

Service is about making sure that we give as much to the community as possible, to ensure that our places and our identity are being nourished and nurtured.

Service for me is knowing that I have a responsibility—my job here is to serve the students, and sometimes that gets me in trouble, because that can be more than is expected of me by my institution.

Because I'm Samoan, respect, honesty, service—those are huge for me.

Service to me is all about just being there for the students, and if something's missing then I'm not serving my purpose of why I'm here. This comes from our home—from any event our rides home were always used by our parents as teaching points, and that's how we grew up knowing what to do.

### How can the value of service help our learners in their learning?

We had a strong Pasifika group of teachers who were upgrading their qualifications who had a strong sense of community—all providing service to the group and each other to help them all succeed. They felt a strong obligation to each other to look after each other and get each other through, and their commitment motivated me to go above and beyond for them as well. Because of their strong commitment to the learning, I did more than usual in many ways. Because of their commitment, I felt going over and above my role was my obligation, but, also, I knew that I was gaining just as much from them in the relationship as they were from me. It was a real relationship of service amongst us all, with tuakana–teina support. Tuakana–teina is a big thing for Cook Islanders—sometimes as a teacher I'll be the teina, because the students know a lot more of the cultural knowledge and protocols than I do. Sometimes I needed their knowledge of these, just as they needed my knowledge of the coursework. As teachers, we all need to see and respect both types of knowledge (cultural and coursework) as valuable and important. Our education system, the curriculum, and assessment for qualifications do not convey this valuing of cultural knowledge and do not promote knowing your own language and culture well, so it is important to be able to learn from our students who have this to help us serve others through our teaching. We worry for our children when they leave the language nests as most schools do not prioritise helping these children continue to develop their cultural understandings and knowledge through their time at school, and the relationships and mutual service that this group had are not yet common.

### How does service play out in our learning environments?

I nurture the value of service by making sure that I am approachable and available. I walk around a lot—I don't just stay in one place in the learning context—so they can ask a quiet question rather than raising their hand if they are too embarrassed to let others know that they are struggling.

To me, service in my teaching is about making sure everyone shares understanding of the programmes we are running with our Tokelauan immersion class and that they can share in what we are doing. As a staff, we talk together about all of our programmes and we all share our ideas about them—everyone knows what everyone is doing. That's important because it builds that notion of community—that's the main thing for us, to hold hands together, know each other, and love each other. We ask the kids to come together as well—greeting people and looking after them, like when we are cooking, we open the door for the parents to come in to share our way to cook and our way of fishing and our weaving. We share the menu we cook—the fish and the talo which is a type of Tokelau food. These occasions help share our cultural understandings of providing food and knowing what's required for some situations; that all comes into our service—for them all to know our way, the way of our people.

Thinking of how I demonstrate service in my teaching, I often collect student voice after every topic to get insight into which of my practices worked for them and which didn't. Before I group them, I ask them to name two students they work well with and a student who could be a friend but who distracts them, so all that helps me with my planning and makes their learning more of a partnership between them and me. I also see service in my teaching as giving varied activities rather than sticking with only one style, and I like to have a routine, so students know what to expect. My students like routines so they know what is coming. With homework, I do the same and just ask them to give me feedback on what they found difficult and what was easy, to inform future planning. Part of my role as a teacher and a fluent Tokelauan speaker in terms of service is promoting Tokelauan and using the Tokelauan language.

Our institution's Pacific leadership group has definitely had service as an area we've tried to continue working on. For example, we just took a group of students to Fiji, leaving them in a village for 3 days—this was partly about helping them understanding what service means, not only for themself, but for others who are not as fortunate.

Universities are historically Eurocentric and have developed in Eurocentric ways. Our institution wants to attract more Pasifika students, but if we really want the Pasifika students to stay and do well, we have to change the way we do things here. In my final assignment for one course, students get into groups and reflect on how well the institution addresses diversity. They have to prepare a presentation for first-year students about the support on offer to them here. They find there are gaps and then they brainstorm ways to address the gaps. For example, one group focused strategies to ensure names are pronounced well at graduation. So, my assessment is also about the everyday lives that they live in centres and schools and how to identify and address gaps. Another group identified the feeling of stereotypes that they see here, like in the different clubs and societies students can join. They talked about going along to these with a friend rather than on their own to help them feel comfortable investigating joining a new group. Their ideas provide service to their friends and the wider Pasifika student community as well as potentially to their institution. I've also used some of these ideas in workshops for various groups and with other institutions. The assignment work is nurturing service in the students because they're coming up with strategies, which they share, using their knowledge, understanding, and experience to make things better for others. The values are woven through the work that we are doing together, but I know I have to keep thinking about ways to demonstrate and nurture the values within my teaching.

### Example in practice: Teaching as service

When we observed the first lecture of a large first-year tertiary course, we saw how teaching can be positioned as providing service for learners. Everything was ready for learners—course materials, readings, tutors, PowerPoint—and there was music to greet them. Students were asked to reflect on why they were taking the course and invited to share their reasons. Lecturer and tutor availability for support was explained and the lecturer and tutors introduced themselves. Students were encouraged to set themselves high expectations and to seek support when needed. They were encouraged to connect with each other and course leaders both verbally and by the open positive body language and interactions of lecturer and tutors. The lecturer told learners that she got up at 5am for them, to be ready to teach. Many opportunities were made during the lecture for students to personally reflect on lecture focus areas and share their perspectives with those close by and with the whole group. These discussion times enabled the lecturer and tutors to get to students to have one-to-one and one-to-small-group conversations.

Respect, family, inclusion, and reciprocal relationships also were demonstrated and nurtured through starting the course in this way.

### How does service relate to the other values?

For us, in order for you to be in a leadership role, you've got to serve and then you'll be able to understand when you get up there, what's going on at the bottom. I do a lot of service. I do a lot of volunteer work; I've done heaps of it. Back in the Islands we just serve, we just love serving—it's just automatic. Because we always say to our young ones in our community, "If you want to be up here, then you have to serve. You have to serve your parents, you have to serve your community, you have to serve anyone in our community to be in a leadership role. You have to earn the right to be a leader."

> *in order for you to be in a leadership role, you've got to serve and then you'll be able to understand when you get up there, what's going on at the bottom.*

What service means for me is that you have to do a lot of the voluntary work—not just paid work. Do a lot of voluntary work and be a good role model. Service is what you give even though you're not getting paid for it, like supporting the family and supporting the community. It comes from your heart because you can make a valuable contribution because you have the skills. Service is offering those things no matter what. I've grown that way. Even though there are challenges, I'm not worried, I want to beat the challenges and learn. Then I can do better.

### What understandings of service are needed in learning environments?

Service is natural to Pacific kids, but it may not be natural to other people who might not understand. For example, when Mr A comes in the classroom, the Pacific kids know straightaway he wants some helpers. You know, they love helping. You'll also find that when you walk around the school at morning tea and lunchtime—if the kids see our caretaker doing something, they go to help him. You know, that's just in them. If they see me and I've got a handful of things, they know, and they just help. They just do it, but that goes both ways because I feel I need to be giving service as an example as well. We want non-Pasifika teachers and kids to understand this noticing of others' needs and giving service, because there is a difference in how we act in these kinds of situations to how many non-Pasifika teachers and children act. They don't have to fully understand our ideas of service to do the actions—the actions are easy to put into practice. But if they don't understand about the giving and the love from a Pacific perspective, then how can the Pacific parents feel very comfortable in this place? And how can the kids learn the best if they're not being treated at school as they're being treated elsewhere?

We have a very strong Pacific student support programme at our institution. We have an assigned support person for different groups of students. Mentors are responsible for running academic support programmes and co-ordinating with course co-ordinators, academics, and students. Funding is from the central university funds. We also have a designated physical space that Pacific students can come to where they can relax and study.

We sadly have fewer Pacific staff than would be ideal, which makes embedding Pacific ways of doing and thinking in our programmes harder to do. Sadly, I cannot say that the faculty has the Pacific values embedded into their work. We do have at least one Pacific academic person in all of the key faculty committees and we have faculty leadership who are attentive and responsive to our requests, as we long as we can provide them with those ideas. I have learned the importance of the academic standing of Pacific academics in bringing in funding for enabling what needs to be done in the Pacific space. Basically, I work hard to get money through projects and I use this for promoting the work academically and to support staff and postgraduate students in ways that I can decide about, with the support of those whose sign-off is needed. My values lead me to work like this—to always work on finding and pursuing how can we make things better, and academic standing and bringing in funding are key to this for me. It's important work and it's rewarding and it's enabling us to create a structure in line with our values. My strategic thinking and planning are driven not by my career or by kudos, but by working on how we as Pacific people can have agency to make decisions about our education ourselves.

In summary, attending to the value of service can involve looking out for others' needs and expectations and attending to these with love, diligence, and prudence. Service is linked to leadership and giving to and supporting others. Service to family can take priority over carrying out personal activities, including learning activities. Pacific parents teach children about service from an early age and children are involved in giving service to others from when they are very young. Educators can serve their learners and learners' families by seeking and using student and parent voice in their decision making and being available to learners and parents.

## Discussion questions

Tasi  How can educators demonstrate and nurture the value of service in their teaching and interactions?

Lua  How can teachers create learning communities that prioritise service to one another's learning and academic progress?

Tolu  How can educators find out, understand, acknowledge, and make allowance for the service their students may be giving to their families and communities?

Fā  How can learning environments serve Pacific parents and families in ways consistent with Pacific perspectives of service?

Lima  How can we honour the expertise of Pacific learners in ways that help all learners understand and value the importance and strengths of providing service?

## Ideas for extra reading

**Family knowledge and practices useful in Tongan boys' education**
Fa'avae (2017)

Focusing on family cultural activities many Tongan males experience, this article discusses the development of service and leadership outside and within formal learning contexts. Findings are drawn from a study involving three generations of males in New Zealand and Tonga.

**Sailiga tomai ma malamalama'aga fa'a-Pasifika—Seeking Pasifika knowledge to support student learning: Reflections on cultural values following an educational journey to Samoa**
Surtees, Tufulasi Taleni, Ismail, Rarere-Briggs, & Stark (2021)

Drawing from experiences of educators on an educational visit to Samoa, the article discusses the importance of educators understanding Pasifika cultural values and integrating these into their practice. It illustrates the affordances of making such a journey for developing these understandings. Tautua, service, and alofa, love are discussed in light of decisions made by hosts and visitors during the visit.

**Pacific university graduates in New Zealand: What helps and hinders completion**
Theodore, Taumoepeau, Tustin, Gollop, Unasa, Kokaua, Taylor, Ramrakha, Hunter, & Poulton (2018)

Pacific graduates across eight New Zealand universities discuss what helped and hindered their studies. Family was frequently seen as what helped and motivated as well as what could hinder gaining of qualifications. Peer support and Pacific academic support groups contributed to success. Service to others including through actioning family responsibilities is discussed as having positive and negative consequences on achievement.

**Service: A deeply meaningful value vital for Pacific learners**
Rimoni, Averill, & Glasgow (2021)

This article highlights Pacific educators' notions of service and how service is pivotal when working with Pacific learners. Ways service can be woven into teaching and learning environments are presented.

**References**

Anae, M. (1997). Towards a NZ-born Samoan identity: Some reflections on 'labels'. *Pacific Health Dialog, 4*(2), 128–137.

Fa'avae, D. (2017). Family knowledge and practices useful in Tongan boys' education. *Set: Research Information for Teachers*, (2), 49–56. : https://doi.org/10.18296/set.0082

Fairburn-Dunlop, T. P. (2010). 'He's won, but he's lost it': Applying a Samoan gender lens to education outcomes. *AlterNative: An International Journal of Indigenous Peoples, 6*(2), 143–154. https://doi.org/10.1177/117718011000600206

Rimoni, F. (2016). *Tama Samoa stories: Experiences and perceptions of identity, belonging and future aspirations at secondary school.* Unpublished PhD thesis, Victoria University of Wellington. https://ojs.victoria.ac.nz/nzaroe/article/download/4151/3668/5394

Rimoni, F. Averill, R., & Glasgow, A. (2021). Service: A deep, meaningful value vital for Pasifika learning. *Set: Research Information for Teachers*, (1), 12–19. https://doi.org/10.18296/set.0192

Surtees, N., Tufulasi Taleni, L., Ismail, R., Rarere-Briggs, B., & Stark, R. (2021). Sailiga tomai ma malamalama'aga fa'a-Pasifika—Seeking Pasifika knowledge to support student learning: Reflections on cultural values following an educational journey to Samoa. *New Zealand Journal of Educational Studies, 56,* 269–283. http://doi.org/10.1007/s40841-021-00210-7

Theodore, R., Taumoepeau, M., Tustin, K., Gollop, M., Unasa, C., Kokaua, J., ... & Poulton, R. (2018). Pacific university graduates in New Zealand: What helps and hinders completion. *AlterNative: An International Journal of Indigenous Peoples, 14*(2), 138–146. https://doi.org/10.1177/1177180118764126

Va'a, U. L. F. (2009). Samoan custom and human rights: An Indigenous view. *Victoria University of Wellington Law Review, 40*(1), 237–240. https://ojs.victoria.ac.nz/vuwlr/article/view/5388

# Educator practice—Demonstrating and nurturing service

| My role | My actions |
|---|---|
| Interacting with learners | Learn about service learners give to others and strengths they can offer. |
| | Discuss with learners about obligations they have at home or in the community that could affect their work completion and homework and accommodate their service. |
| | Encourage all learners to be of service to each other, including in meeting learning goals, and to understand that service builds community. |
| | Use a rota of teacher and learner helpers. |
| | Explain your own volunteer work and support learners' involvement in community. |
| Interacting with parents and families | As an educator, team, or institution, facilitate conversations with families about service in order to explore and acknowledge the responsibilities learners and families have. |
| Planning | Give learners opportunities to assist one another and expect them to. |
| | Plan times where learners can learn together. |
| | Understand that community involvement may be more important to learners and families than their activities in learning contexts, due to cultural expectations, and plan for flexibility. |
| Teaching | Use examples of your own community involvement in your teaching. Model service by modelling and discussing that educators often take on extra roles in the school like coaching teams and taking learners on visits out of the learning context. |
| | Use service to others as a context for learning experiences. |
| Celebrating | Acknowledge and recognise learners who provide service in the learning context or community. |
| | Distribute community awards for involvement. |
| Assessing and reporting | Be thoughtful and reflective when giving feedback and be aware of potential implications for learners and families of the feedback given. |
| | Acknowledge learners' service in reporting. |
| | Provide opportunities for parents to initiate assessment conversations and give feedforward and feedback on teaching programmes. |
| Being an advocate for my Pacific colleagues, Pacific learners, and their families | Encourage the administration to acknowledge and cater for learners' and Pacific colleagues' service in processes, policies, and expectations. |

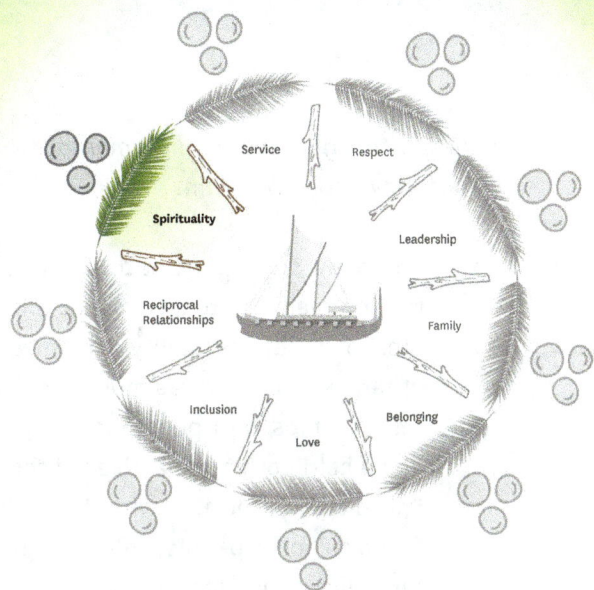

Chapter Six

# Spirituality

**What does spirituality mean to Pacific people? How can learning environments recognise and acknowledge Pacific perspectives of spirituality?**

> *A'oa'o ia i le tama e tusa ma lona ala; a o'o ina toeaina lava o ia, e le te'a ese ai.*
> *Faataoto 22: 6*

> *Train a child in the way he should go; and when he is old, he will not depart from it.*
> *Proverbs 22: 6*

We would like to say fa'afetai tele lava, thank you very much, to the Samoan community of the EFKS Church and A'oga Amata (Samoan language nest) Newtown. The Aoga Amata was founded by the Minister Ete and his wife Fereni, to ensure that Samoan children would learn Gagana and Fa'a Samoa (Samoan language, cultural practices, and values) in the language nest. The church community was pivotal in establishing the Aoga Amata and the connection continues today, with consultation with the church community in selecting this proverb and *with spiritual guidance a fundamental principle within the Aoga Amata philosophy and curriculum.*

- Spirituality is important to all of the Pacific educators we spoke to; however, spirituality meant different things to different people. To some, spirituality was linked to their Christian faith. For others, spirituality was more about intangible aspects of life and relationships with people in the present and who have passed. Some held both perspectives of the value.
- Spirituality associated with the Christian faith can be very deeply felt by Pacific people, affecting them from birth and baptism throughout their life.
- Learners being able to be strong in themselves and their cultural identity are seen as important aspects of spirituality.

Spirituality, which can be thought of as a yearning for being connected to something larger than ourselves, is a contributor to mental health and wellbeing and has an important place in effective teaching and education (Palmer, 2003; Toso, 2011). The term "spirituality" describes consideration of the transcendent dimension of human experience, with the concept of institution-based religion—a relatively recent development—encompassed within the idea of spirituality (Ai, 2002). Indigenous knowledge includes the beliefs, spirituality, arts, practices, and other forms of cultural and traditional experiences that belong to Indigenous communities, all important to preserve and promote within education (Ali, 2017; Kalavite, 2020). Heritage languages are key to these aspects of identity, yet diminishing capabilities with the languages of their forbears, exacerbated by our largely monolingual education system, is a deep concern of many New Zealand-born Pacific people (Samu et al., 2019).

Ancient Polynesians believed in Tangaroa, Rangi, Rongo, Tane, and many other gods. Some believed in a great god 'Io and another god whose name was too tapu to say. 'Io, who lived in the highest heaven at the heart of creation, could be understood only through the priests (Makirere, 2003). Polynesians saw objects as physical containers that the gods entered on appropriate occasions and then left to return to the spirit world. The ancient Polynesian gods had well-defined roles and attributes. Chants describe evolution through total darkness until 'Io spoke and told the darkness to become light, and light to contain darkness (Makirere, 2003). Awareness and consideration of the traditional gods varies amongst Pacific people, but practices such as giving the first fish caught back to Tangaroa persist with some families and communities.

There are many ways of thinking about and considering spirituality outside and within educational settings, even through respecting the silences and quietness that spiritual wellbeing and peace can bring (Toso, 2011). Discussing spirituality brought out deep emotions and varied views across our Pacific educator interviews. Commonalities include that most Pacific people hold strong beliefs and spirituality is tied for many with feelings of community, family, faith, service, and belonging.

Let's hear from our Pacific educators ...

### What does spirituality mean to you?

So, spirituality to me is your connection with the outside world. We know through our upbringing, it's us and God. Culture and religion run parallel—you can't run one without the other.

Spirituality is part of everything. Every part of your living moment is about spirituality really —for Pacific or Polynesian people it's just built into how we think. That's a benefit of the language nests because spirituality is inherent in how things are done. We do our karakia or lotu in the morning and the students experience that when they start the day, and the sense of spiritual connection goes right through their day. At mat time there are often songs, hymns, and children will do their pepeha, so they're connecting to their ancestors and to their world. There are a lot of blessings that are included, more than would happen in an English-medium setting. That spirituality and that spiritual realm is built into the children's world and it's fostered in them.

My understanding of spirituality is religion and my religion is Catholicism, so I'm Catholic and this was instilled in me from my grandparents. Every evening Monday to Saturday at 6 o'clock, we went to a village house and did the rosary—we did all of that and then sang the hymn. Sunday was church, 9 o'clock mass and we had a long way to walk to church, so that and the teachings of the Catholic church to me is spirituality. Spirituality stems around God and church, prayer and meditation. We were poor so we always prayed that things would be provided, and they always were. In a hurricane or anything like that, it was always prayer that gets us through. Now I'm reading for my research I know that spirituality is wider than that, but in my Fijian context, I didn't know so much about spirituality of the cosmos and the land and more. There is an acceptance now of a wider understanding of spirituality. I hear about the myths and things, but pre-Christian understandings of spirituality were never a part of my upbringing or thinking. What I'm learning now and reading about traditional Fijian views, I'm linking with Māori to understand it because I knew of Māori myths but not Fijian ones, so now I'm like, "Oh, this one's like the Māori story of the beginning."

When I think spirituality, I think Christianity. From the moment we were born, that is what we know. We were prayed over; we were baptised. We grew up in Sunday school so that is our first formal education before entering school.

Church was the constant source of strength and spirituality in our life. I still live by that today. I've often thought, with all these new evangelical churches that spring up, I just say to myself, "No, if the traditional church worked for my grandparents back then, that is what I'm going to practice" and keep going because for my family, it's something constant. To me the church is the constant and the foundation. When I was on my OE, in times of hardship, I knew where to go to. I knew there was always something that I could do, I would go to church, I would say a prayer. There is always the "go to" that helps me feel connected and know there is a wider purpose, that tomorrow will be better. There is a sense of calm after that, so there is always hope, or there is always a light when I have a religious aspect to me. After all, who really knows what is right? But I know for me, this is right for me, and this is what I will do, so I'm keeping with that.

On the island I'm from, which is part Fijian and part Tongan, we could call sharks. Our thing was that we called sharks and they'd come and swim with us and then we'd fish them. That was our thing, but I never really knew about doing that. I just know of Christianity, because it came to the islands and my grandparents just took to it, and everything was prayer and that was their survival. So, to me, spirituality is about the Bible and our morals and how we do things in our religion.

There is the Christian church aspect of spirituality and there is more than that as well. We're not just people walking around on the planet—there is a purpose and a bigger meaning to life which I think a lot of Pasifika people find through church and through God. There is also a wider aspect—like the Samoan culture is not individualistic, it is much more community-minded, living life and doing life together, and that is a spiritual thing. It is like we are connected and that there is more than just the physical tangible aspect of what we share.

A spiritual experience doesn't have to be a dogma—instead, it's how we as citizens of this society and this community react to and care for each other. That's a spiritual relationship underpinned by values.

### In terms of teaching and the learning environment, how does demonstrating and nurturing spirituality play out?

Spirituality. My initial thoughts about the value of spirituality were that we'll talk about God, but then I reflected back—when I was a student teacher and I had my final practicum at a Catholic school—and we're not Catholic. I worried that I don't know much about Catholic practices but from that experience I learnt that spirituality is more than the religious way of understanding. It encompassed wellbeing. It was about your attention to other people, how you care for other people, your behaviour, your manners, and about relating to not only people but to the environment, even the furniture within a class. It is all those things and how you respect everything around you. So, I believe that spirituality connects well across all the Pacific values but it connects tightly with respect in terms of how you treat others and

> *spirituality connects well across all the Pacific values but it connects tightly with respect in terms of how you treat others and other objects and the environment and your surroundings*

other objects and the environment and your surroundings—looking after these things will come back in their way of looking after you. Spirituality is about connecting to that care and that manner that you have, but it's not just between humans, it's about everything—with a holistic overview of looking at yourself and anyone else.

The Pasifika families at our learning context put any differences aside. We belong to different organisations and churches, but we are Niuean. We have never had any feedback that a child can't come into the mat time, the spiritual time.

In our school pōwhiri we always have a Māori speaker, a Samoan speaker, and the Principal or DP as the English speaker and the kids sing the Pese lotu which is kind of like a hymn, which is a renowned song in the school. The teachers know the translation of it and that's the starting point of spirituality in our school.

In the classroom, I have to be wary and tread carefully, because of the way the world is these days and the different types of religions. It shuts you down from embedding your beliefs in your class, but at our school a lot of these kids come from the same background—whether it's Catholic or AOG or whatever. Kids know that, before we eat, they have to do grace, whether it's quiet or out loud. The Samoan kids know that, when it comes to lunch or morning tea, they're saying the lotu that we're used to, the Malie pule. The Pālagis are like, "Wow, I want to learn that chant", and I go, "Hey, it's not a chant." We're quite wary of a backlash from parents about religious things, but we do it in our language nest, I do it in my class, and so the kids just freely do it because at lunch time they all meet up out there. You can hear the Samoan kids know it and do it, but then you have other kids who are like, "Oh, I want to learn that rhyme." It's cool hearing more and more, but actually understanding the deeper meaning of what they're doing is important and then they go home and say "Oh, I learnt this" so it can be tricky. You feel you want to include more on the spiritual side, but you also feel you have blocks in front of you doing that.

This is not something I thought much about before in relation to the learning context. I am a Christian but working in a secular job where spirituality is not something that we would talk about openly in teaching, or even with other staff. However, educators understanding Pacific perspectives on spirituality will help them understand where Pacific people are coming from in their actions and interactions, and the way that they think about the world. Thinking about it, in the learning context, the basic ways of relating to each other, like respecting the other person, not being selfish, and valuing others are really fundamental things that do come from a place of spirituality. I think these ideas of attending to spirituality are tied together with helping ensure learners' wellbeing, their sense of self, and their learning potential, by showing that you truly believe that everybody is worthy and everybody and every learner has potential. Every learner can do more than they did yesterday. When you believe that, that is going to make a difference to your teaching and help the students feel positive about themselves. Valuing others also helps you to respect whatever it is that students and parents bring, because there are so many religious beliefs, cultures, socioeconomic situations, and knowing about and being able to honour all of those aspects of people is really important.

I see nurturing of spirituality being played out in Catholic schools by them talking about Catholic character or virtues. They're all good things to have instilled in you and are not just based on religion. They still focus on what we as Catholics do but there's more emphasis on talking about virtues and being a good servant person and what that looks like, so it's inclusive of everyone who might not be so hard-out Catholic. The teaching is compatible with the teachings of the Bible, but without teaching the Bible.

### How is the value of spirituality part of your work?

Our school values align with gospel values—kindness, serving and service, leadership, working together, and using restorative practice of not punishing but talking it out and making things right by doing the right thing.

I look at myself and I think a lot of the parents of these kids now are my generation, and for a lot of that generation the language is lost, so they've come out like Pālagi Samoan, so the values they were given when they were young have changed and they're lost. A lot of the kids in my class are here from parent requests—a lot of the Samoan parents have requested for their kids to come in here because they know that I float in and out of the mother tongue, and even the Pālagi kids and the Māori kids pick it up. That's me—if you don't want to hear it, go and find another classroom.

We use religious protocols; like when we have our Polyclub practice, our leaders ask who wants to volunteer to do the prayers, and we end the practice with a prayer as well. Even when it comes to games, we ask for God's blessing. It seems weird when you are in a Pacific gathering if you don't start with a prayer. It is acknowledgement of God and what God has provided and asking his blessing on what we are going to do together. We feel more comfortable about whatever it is that we are doing when we have started with a prayer having attended to those things that matter first. Just like at any Pacific gathering, we have food and it doesn't feel right without that, or without blessing the food and the people who prepared it before we eat. So, if we have food at school, it needs to be the norm that food is provided for gatherings and that the food is blessed. When attending to protocols enables everybody to feel comfortable, then we don't want to start events without that.

Pacific parents I've spoken to want their kids to have an emphasis on spirituality in school so that they get the opportunity there to explore their spirituality. One parent discussed this in terms of their kids having the opportunity to explore their spiritualities in relation to whether they have enjoyment in something or whether they feel good about themselves, so that's got different implications for teaching than the other ideas about spirituality. It is more about making each learner feel okay to be themselves and welcomed and respected.

The White Sunday ceremonies are an example of how spirituality has been adapted to a Christian approach—in our language nest, families were all involved and, even though a lot of the younger parents don't generally go to church, they brought their children in for that day so they could understand this is part of their culture. Even if they come in just for that occasion, it's bringing them back to a connection to a spiritual aspect of their lives.

*Are there other sides to spirituality, other than the Christian and faith side?*

Spirituality is not Christianity per say although as Pacific people many of us have embraced Christianity wholeheartedly because we can connect to the spiritual element of it. But there's more to our thinking about spirituality than church and religion. For example, I was just thinking last week when my cousin had passed away how the notion of dreams is really important to us—I'd had a dream the night before he died that I was going off to Rarotonga and I was saying, "I don't want to go, I don't want to go." I don't know why I didn't want to go, but I got a call early that morning to say that my cousin had passed away and that they were taking him back to Rarotonga. My mother always used to have a dream about something significant before it happened and I don't know whether it's spirituality or something else, but we can have that sense that something is going to be happening. Often when the body passes, there may be a visit before they head off to where they need to be going when they pass. So, for me, spirituality is also around that idea that those who have passed on are still here. The spiritual guides are here even when they have passed. That was brought home to me when we took my Mum back to her island. My uncle was still alive, and we went to sleep down on her land and we said, "Well, probably grandma will visit us tonight." It is a normal part of how we think and what we expect. It's just part of who we are as a people; it's almost that sixth sense or just knowing that that spiritual realm is all around us.

Some parents talk about spirituality in ways some other people might think of as spooky. For example, one New Zealand-born Samoan second-generation parent I've talked with has a real take on the spiritual side of Fa'asamoa, and his first thoughts are about spirit world, what comes after life. The spirit world ideas are quite strong in a Samoan sense. He's gone through experiences with family members relating to the spirit world. I didn't feel comfortable talking about that, but in listening to his stories, he talked about it being a good thing that you have that understanding of the other world. Other Pacific people feel like it's evil and that we shouldn't be going there, and we should leave it alone. From their perspective, you don't go there—you know that they're there, but you don't go there. Some Pacific authors talk about the spiritual world and there are certain stories about spirit women who would try to lead men in their worlds. He talked about the spirit world as a beautiful thing, but if you were to go and talk to someone else about it, like an elder, they will chastise you for saying that.

My Mum would share stories around people she grew up with who were told they were ill, but at the end of the day, they were seeing spirits—this is a common Samoan perspective. There are certain places when we go to Samoa that we never go to because of those stories. We just leave it alone. There are places you go, there are things you say, but there are other things you just leave.

There's more awareness of the spirit world in the Pasifika community than the non-Pacific community. The feelings and the terms used differ as well. You'll hear non-Pacific people talk about ghosts, and on the TV you've got some Europeans chasing ghosts, and you're thinking, "How could they do that?" You would never see someone go and record and do a video or a documentary around those things in a Pacific country, it's just tapu. You just don't go there. There are certain people who can deal with those things in our community, that's just what they do.

### How do you nurture spirituality with your students?

We prepare our student teachers through teaching and modelling. For example, we teach them about starting sessions with karakia and waiata and we do these with them. We will always say a karakia before we have our food and often start mat time with a karakia. I also always start with a whakataukī and make a connection to our tangata whenua. These are to get them prepared for when they're in early childhood centres and schools. I think it's important to acknowledge with them that we're all spiritual beings in our own ways and it may not necessarily be from a Polynesian perspective for everyone, but just to connect that part of our lives is important for us.

I always say to my students, "Look, being culturally responsive is a bit like thinking of the zone of proximal development—we just need to keep making little steps to move forward, manageable steps." The sense of achievement when you move up to the next step is huge and then you can build on that, but I tell them not to try and do it all at once, because that's impossible and that's not what we would want of them. For our student teachers, the cultural stuff is often the hardest stuff. They don't want to offend anyone, but they have to just make the first move and consult and learn and continue. Having good communication is key and they'll find that people and parents are really willing to give. Our students saw this in the language nests, saying things like, "Wow, this is amazing! They were so helpful!" As a consequence, I have students asking almost every year if they can have a teaching placement in Samoa or the Cook Islands. If they're showing this interest, then being immersed in the culture like that would be fantastic—to be the minority in those places, they would learn so much about spirituality and the other values in practice.

### Example in practice: Celebrating cultural identity

Cook Island song and dance were playing on a video as students came into the learning space. A Cook Island cloth covered the table at the front of the room. The educator, a Cook Islander herself, was wearing Cook Island dress, jewellery, had her hair in a bun—traditional for many older Pacific women—and headwear. Students were greeted with Cook Island greetings, kia orana, as they arrived, and the teaching began with a mihimihi and links to Cook Island language week activities. A whakataukī was introduced and explained in terms of the ethics of drawing from this proverb, and key ideas of the day's learning were linked to it through discussion. The teaching began with a video of a Cook Island children's dance, then linked to teaching key points. Gentle, humble ways were used to encourage co-operation and respect for others, including through teaching about the Cook Island virtues of integrity, fidelity, humility, and public spiritedness.

Providing a learning context so rich in Cook Island ways of being and doing links to learners' sense of identity, both for Cook Island heritage learners and others, enhancing their cultural identities and understanding, and opening the way for conversations and sharing of cultural knowledge and expertise. By teaching in this way, the educator shared much of herself, her family, and community. Along with spirituality, this teaching demonstrated respect, belonging, inclusion, and love.

Spirituality is quite hard for some of our student teachers to get their head around because many have been raised in a secular way. Many don't go to church and that's almost seen as a scary thing. It is important for these student teachers to be open, develop a mindset of openness, and react from the heart—that's a sort of a spiritual experience that can certainly be achieved and will make a difference for learners.

We talked about the spirit world in class, about tohunga and what their role was—they deal with the spiritual world and attend to things that need to be attended to. We all do what has to be done to clear matters or make pathways, so there are also those feelings about spirituality that would not be commonly thought about in our school environments. The spirit world is definitely a common perspective and every culture, or every ethnicity, has their stories of what that means for them.

### What is it like for our Pasifika learners in settings where there is little attention to spirituality?

Thinking back to my own experience of being a school student in the 1960s, I had to learn to compartmentalise my life, because I was raised with spirituality being part of our lives. My Mum was very spiritual, and we were Christian, but the spiritual emphasis was missing at school. At school, we learnt that you acted in the school's way and what you were required to do, and that part of your life wasn't even a part of your school life. School wasn't a place where I could connect to my family life, and I learnt to push that part of my life out of the way at school. My parents knew that was what the expectation was, but looking back, we saw at school that a big part of our lives wasn't seen as important. It's probably much the same today for many Pasifika learners.

My mokopuna has just started school; he's just 5 and my daughter put on his enrolment form that he is Cook Island Māori. He came home on the first or second day and said, "I'm a Cook Islander". The teacher must have looked at his form and we thought, "Wow, that's the first time that anyone in my family has come home and said that, so maybe things are changing in schools a bit." He is in a very multicultural low-decile school, and we think that's going to be a good thing for him because he will grow up with a sense that we are a really culturally diverse society and be comfortable with people from different groups. I think that it's a blessing for him and my other moko who look quite Polynesian. Their best mates are Māori and Pacific boys and they've got access to a cultural connection with the children at their schools. That teacher's actions show that there is the capacity to enhance children's sense of identity in school, but how they do this is up to each individual teacher who will either decide this is important or it's not—so it is hit and miss for our Pacific children because it doesn't always happen. Our education system promotes that we still live in a white privilege world, unwittingly and unconsciously, but unconscious bias comes through in our actions as teachers, so if we can dismantle that in practical ways, like acknowledging ethnicity, it's going to be hugely beneficial for our children, our students.

### How do languages connect with spirituality?

Language connections are really important; we have a range of different mother tongues. Even though English is the language that we all speak together, having another language is so special. Language helps you know who you are and gives us a sense of belonging.

Teaching for me is easier in the Niuean immersion class because I am quite fluent in the language. This is the first time that we've had a whole Niuean class, and this is big for us. I'm lucky that I've got also a Niuean colleague and we've got some of the matuas from the community who come in and help out. This initiative is driven from the community; they wanted for a long time to have a whole Niuean class in usual school time. When we ran out of funding for the Niuean after-school programme, the development stopped for a while, but then we carried it on without pay or anything, just with the little bit of money that was left. So, I'm just glad our class is during school time now. The children are making great progress. One of the parents is asking if the Niue class is going to continue next year or not, because she can see the difference in her daughter. Her daughter is more confident at home. She goes home, they sing the songs, and she even shares her pepeha. We've got Year 2 to Year 4 children and that is a big range for me. But after Year 4, we don't know if there's going to be a follow-on class for these kids. We're really pushing for another Niue teacher and hopefully there's going to be one, because the children have learnt a lot of the language and they're using it. To go back into the mainstream classes would be sad. Having this immersion class is huge for us—being able to teach them our culture, our way. They want to know where they come from and there are a lot of things that I can pass on to the kids.

In our school, some Tongan parents choose the Tongan language unit for their children and others choose the mainstream classes. It is good they have the choice according to what their child needs and what will suit their child and their family. Some of the children in my immersion class are not yet strong in the Tongan language and I say to the children, "Listen carefully, everyone makes mistakes." I encourage them. Some of them are shy to say something. I say to them, "How do you know you're right or wrong until you just bring it out? I make a lot of mistakes. Don't think the teacher knows everything. Everyone makes mistakes." I tell them, "There's only one person who is perfect—the one up there."

Normally, we have a Tongan lotu in the morning and we have the kai time. We start to bring in the Tongan ways of doing things, but we teach those strengths slowly, bit by bit. The first things we focus on are our values. We talk about respect. Bringing in the lotu is the first thing for us, then I talk about the lotu, and I tell them to listen carefully when I say the lotu. They should be thinking about the words. I say, "So if you sit without focusing on the lotu, do you think he can hear you?" For some of the kids, the parents take them to church for their understanding and that's why I talk with them about it. I say, "Think about the words you talk about—ask for the strength, ask for the knowledge, ask for the light in you. Think about it. If you're going to sit here and your mind is all over the place, do you think he's going to hear you? No. Just talk and think about it." That's what I'm saying when I teach them about lotu. In my teaching, I keep everyone together—if I can see any behaviour or something that's going to distract the others, I stop teaching. I put them together and talk, and after that they go back to their work.

In summary, attending to the value of spirituality can mean educating each learner in the ways they should be and travel through life, so that they can experience the strengths of these ways throughout their lives. Spirituality can be about connection with others, religion, God or gods, and values. Spirituality can be all-encompassing, governing protocols such as lotu and ceremonies and events such as White Sunday. Spirituality connects with caring for others, wellbeing, the environment, and identity. Attending to spirituality means knowing about and acknowledging deeper meanings to songs, chants, and experiences and intangible experiences difficult to understand and explain.

## Discussion questions

Tasi   *What are your understandings of Pacific perspectives of spirituality? How do these compare with your own perspectives?*

Lua   *How can learning environments accommodate and reflect Christian and other perspectives of spirituality?*

Tolu   *How can learning environments and educators nurture students' knowledge and understanding of their Pacific background and cultural identity?*

## Ideas for extra reading

**Integrating spirituality into professional education: A challenging but feasible task**
Ai (2002)

Spiritual beliefs influence attitudes toward one's wellbeing. This article examines the benefits of integrating spirituality into education in relation to enhancing wellbeing. Values, ethics, connections between religion and spirituality, and using spirituality for making connections between people are discussed.

**Teaching with heart and soul: Reflections on spirituality in teacher education**
Palmer (2003)

This article explores the place of spirituality in effective teaching. The article discusses how teachers can demonstrate spiritual ways of being, see potential in their students, and to do more for them than a usual teaching role would involve. Pedagogy of the soul is discussed as a way of teachers creating safe spaces for learners to explore their inner lives and deep understandings of who they are as learners, and who they could become.

**Reconceptualising spirituality as a philosophy of practice for Pasifika early childhood education in New Zealand: A Samoan perspective**
Toso (2011)

This writing presents Samoan views of spirituality and changes in these over time. Pedagogical methods relevant for early childhood education in New Zealand to develop learners' experiences of spirituality, from a Samoan lens, are presented. These can lead to a holistic culturally inclusive approach to teaching. The discussion demonstrates the importance of teachers taking responsibility for children's wellbeing spirituality as well as physically, emotionally, and cognitively.

**Toungāue cooperative pedagogy for Tongan tertiary students' success**
Kalavite (2020)

Tongan beliefs, values, and ways of being and learning are presented in this article which proposes a toungāue—co-operative work approach used in Tongan communities as an approach for tertiary teaching. The discussion is drawn from an extensive study involving tertiary educators and 25 tertiary students in one New Zealand university, all competent Tongan and English speakers and all experienced in the New Zealand education system.

**Tu'utu'u le upega i le loloto—Cast the net into deeper waters: Exploring dance as a culturally sustaining mathematics pedagogy**
Taeao & Averill (2019)

This article draws from a range of literature to argue for using dance such as the sāsā as a pedagogy for developing curriculum knowledge and understanding, with dance connecting to learners' passions, expertise, and emotional and physical wellbeing.

## References

Ai, A. L. (2002). Integrating spirituality into professional education: A challenging but feasible task. *Journal of Teaching in Social Work, 22*(1-2), 103-130. https://doi.org/10.1300/J067v22n01_08

Ali, W. (2017). An Indigenous academic perspective to preserving and promoting Indigenous knowledge and traditions: A Fiji case study. *The Australian Journal of Indigenous Education, 46*(1), 80-91. https://doi.org/10.1017/jie.2016.25

Kalavite, T. (2020). Toungāue cooperative pedagogy for Tongan tertiary students' success. *Waikato Journal of Education, 25*(1), 17-29. https://doi.org/10.15663/wje.v25i0.783

Makirere, T. (2003). 'Irinaki'anga: Changing beliefs and practices. In R. Crocombe & M. Crocombe (Eds.), *Cook Islands culture: Akono'anga Māori*. University of the South Pacific.

Palmer, P. J. (2003). Teaching with heart and soul: Reflections on spirituality in teacher education. *Journal of Teacher Education, 54*(5), 376-385. https://doi.org/10.1177/0022487103257359

Samu, L. V., Barnes, H. M., Asiasiga, L., & McCreanor, T. (2019). "We are not privileged enough to have that foundation of language": Pasifika young adults share their deep concerns about the decline of their ancestral/heritage languages in Aotearoa New Zealand. *AlterNative, 15*(2), 131-139. https://doi.org/10.1177/1177180119835228

Taeao, S., & Averill, R. (2019). Tu'utu'u le upega i le loloto—Cast the net into deeper waters: Exploring dance as a culturally sustaining mathematics pedagogy. *Australian Journal of Indigenous Education, 50*(1), 127-135. https://doi.org/10.1017/jie.2019.17

Toso, V. M. (2011). Reconceptualising spirituality as a philosophy of practice for Pasifika early childhood education in New Zealand: A Samoan perspective. *Pacific-Asian Education Journal, 23*(2), 129-138.

## Educator practice—Demonstrating and nurturing spirituality

| My role | My actions |
|---|---|
| **Interacting with learners** | Be open-minded to diverse spiritual backgrounds, priorities, and practices. |
| | Learn about learners in relation to their spiritual practices and beliefs. |
| | React from the heart. |
| | Encourage learners to meet expectations and strive to achieve their learning and other goals. |
| | Discuss and encourage mutual respect, being selfless, and honouring each other's differences. |
| | Invite discussions about learners' cultural practices. |
| **Interacting with parents and families** | Invite parents to share about the church they may belong to. |
| | Develop understanding of the different churches. |
| | Ask parents to share favourite lotu, pure, or song for use in the learning context. |
| **Planning** | Learn simple prayers and blessings in Pacific languages. |
| | Be cognisant of tapu matters, such as ghosts, and be sensitive to these. |
| **Teaching** | Include kindness, service, leadership, working together, and use themes such as restorative practice in teaching and learning, mirroring the values taught in church. |
| **Celebrating** | Include prayers and blessings in formal occasions and class celebrations. |
| | Invite students to say prayers and blessings in their choice of language. |
| **Being an advocate for my Pacific colleagues, Pacific learners, and their families** | Invite local church leaders to talk. |
| | Attend church services attended by your learners, take food (e.g., packet of biscuits) and stay for kaikai and discussion if invited. |

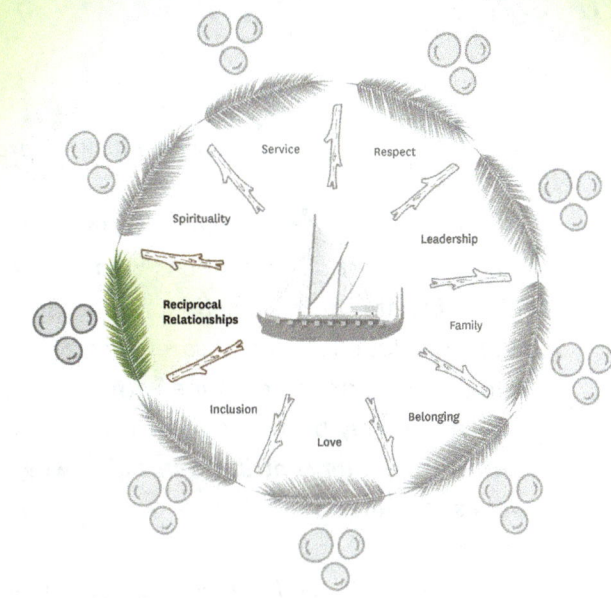

Chapter Seven

# Reciprocal relationships

**What are Pacific people's experiences of and expectations about reciprocal relationships? How can learning environments demonstrate and nurture Pacific perspectives of reciprocal relationships?**

*Images: Dr Tanya Wendt Samu*

*A quiet grove of coconut trees in Nauru. Tall, older trees encircle, nurture, and protect young sprouting trees. Older trees produced the coconuts, that fell to the ground and sprouted.*

## Relationships (reciprocal)

*My parents taught me that responsibility, duty, and service should be at the heart of interactions with others. They taught me that relationships are not transactional. I learned I have the responsibility to nurture relationships and carefully attend to interactions. They taught me that if someone gifts me with their time and support, I am obligated to do my best to look for ways I can support or honour them in turn—if I cannot contribute straight away, I must look out for opportunities at a later point. This is reciprocity. Reciprocity cannot be forced or demanded.*

We very warmly thank Dr Tanya Wendt Samu, a senior lecturer in the Faculty of Education and Social Work at the University of Auckland, for this contribution about reciprocal relationships. Fa'afetai tele lava.

- Attending to reciprocal relationships is usual and important for many Pacific people.
- Everyone gives to others, knowing that they will receive at some point in some way.
- Educators can use reciprocity to advance student engagement and achievement.
- Knowing learners well and having strong relationships with learners enhances educators' opportunities to provide for and support their learners, and to expect reciprocity in their learners attending to tasks.
- The relational spaces between people, the concept of vā, is important for understanding, nurturing, and enacting respectful reciprocal relationships.

Strong positive relationships are key to Pacific learner achievement and wellbeing. In this chapter we explore how, for many Pacific people, reciprocity is an essential and expected part of forging and nourishing strong relationships. We hear how reciprocity can be experienced, enhance relationships, and lead to providing to others what is needed and receiving support when in need oneself. Reciprocity can be as simple as acknowledging one another and as complex as an extended family and community pooling resources to support a family member in need.

Respectful reciprocal relationships with learners and family are key to maximising learning, acknowledging and affirming identity, and considering the languages and cultures of Pacific learners within curriculum implementation (Hunter et al., 2016). Important for such relationships is understanding the notion of vā and protecting the relational spaces between people that recognise the importance of inter-personal and inter-group relationships and responsibilities (Reynolds, 2018; Thaman, 2008). Recognising there are many culturally linked ways of seeing the world and using cross-cultural resources, understandings, and competencies can assist with developing strong reciprocal relationships for learning (Mila-Schaaf & Robinson, 2010).

Let's hear from our Pacific educators ...

### *What does the value reciprocal relationships mean to you?*

Reciprocal relationships are important for the triangle of learning—with the learner in the middle, you have to have all those stakeholders around them, so building the relationships across the group is really important.

Reciprocal relationships is about everybody having worth and everybody having a place, and relationships growing out of that. It helps with knowing you are valued, and you are important in whatever sphere you're in. Reciprocal relationships could be in the older person or the younger person both knowing who they are, both able to participate and interact, like in the talanoa concept. Reciprocal relationships are present in our back and forth and round and round ways of interacting. There is never a one-way approach, nothing fixed or pre-determined. With reciprocal relationships in place, there is living and breathing and growing and changing.

In a relationship, both people have got something to give and have worth. What each person has to say and what each has to bring to that relationship is important, even though your roles or ages may be different, all of those are valued.

The value of reciprocal relationships is a very strong value for Pacific people. It's in the fact that if we give you something, there's that knowledge that something will be delivered in return. An example of that would be with my research—if I work with a community, then the expectation is that I will help them. For example, I'm looking to explore the expertise that the group holds, and in return I've helped with policy writing and with guiding appraisal work because that's expertise that I bring. At a community level, reciprocal relationships in action is about giving being an expectation, and from giving, things will come back to you. I liken it to the concept of ako, where we recognise that both groups have strengths and skills that we can draw on and so we give—we give what we can.

That value for me is all about "what you give, you hope to get back in return". We've been brought up in the church and it's something that we see a lot in the church. Some people say that in Samoan churches all you hear is people giving all their money. I've been part of a church environment for over 40 years and I must admit I said the same to my parents when I was younger, "Why are you giving so much? What are we getting out of it?" But, when our Dad died, they just came, the support was there. That's an example of reciprocal relationships—support comes back to you—it won't necessarily come immediately, but it comes.

> As Pacific people, we've just taken on all this Western stuff in education and we're entrenched in it, and there needs to be more emphasis on Pacific knowledge and ways of being in return.

Reciprocal relationships is around knowing that what we give away will come back to us. In education, we need to turn things around a little bit so that reciprocal relationships can be more strongly present in learning settings. As Pacific people, we've just taken on all this Western stuff in education and we're entrenched in it, and there needs to be more emphasis on Pacific knowledge and ways of being in return. For many Pacific people in education, there's Western stuff we can't move past, like deadlines and policies, but some of these go against the way we feel we should be doing things as a Pacific person. As educators, we need to keep giving examples of how Pacific perspectives can be better catered for. It's a journey that we're all taking together really, isn't it?

*In a learning environment, how can teachers demonstrate and nurture reciprocal relationships?*

Teachers can demonstrate and nurture reciprocal relationships through recognising that, when students walk in the door, they are not empty vessels; they bring so much with them. It is up to the teacher to draw those things the students bring out so they can be recognised, valued, and encouraged in the person. So, rather than the teacher starting from a point of "I am the one who knows everything and you guys need to be told it and learn it all", instead having an approach of "Let's do this together, let's learn this together, what do you already know about it? This is something that I have learnt about that as well, so how could we join all that knowledge together?" So, for me, often there needs to be an introduction to a new method or a new concept, but once students have some understanding, they can really take off and explain things themselves or explain things to others. This comes from a place of recognising that they already have so much. Seeing them outside of the classroom, like playing sports or in musical or cultural performing, or looking after a sibling, helps you realise that. These things help you see them as a whole person.

Reciprocal relationships for me is that two-way thing. I've found that if I am going out of my way to form a relationship with my students, that anytime I need them to do something, they are more than happy to reciprocate. For example, I have students in my maths class who were not doing so well in their previous maths class. For one of them, their teacher was saying they were not going to pass because they were not showing interest in wanting to engage in the learning. That teacher wanted this student to get Level 2 and leave school. I believed this student could aim for Level 3 and had him come into my class and do Level 3. I've not seen any non-engagement. I think it is because I have taken him in and believe in him. When I ask him for a favour outside of the classroom, he is like, "Yeah, sure Miss, I can do that." Taking that step of inviting and accepting him into my class and taking the time to give him another chance and an opportunity, he now wants to give back. There have been many cases like that here, so that idea of reciprocal relationships inside and outside the classroom goes a long way to promote achievement. Some teachers ask, "Why are you giving these kids another chance?" My reply is, "That's our job. It is our job to keep trying to push these kids. They are not ready for the big world, they are not ready to leave." I feel so strongly: "Why settle for Level 2 when they are capable of more?" I think some students can't be at or give their best when values they are used to are not present in teachers' actions.

I like the term "funds of knowledge" and recognising that children come to the learning setting with a lot of wider knowledge—knowledge of their families and connections they have to their communities. As a teacher I look to see what children have in terms of their interests and strengths and what their families and communities surround them with. I use all that in my planning. I can't teach without knowing the wider worlds of the learners. I try to go deep to have a strong understanding of their cultural background—if I don't have that understanding, then I'm not going to be able to work effectively.

In terms of my teaching, if I'm asking a question, I expect that some students or most students would respond. It's a giving back. We have this discussion at home about our work environments, like trying to figure out the best way for my sister to get her team to be on board, or to help our students meet our expectations of their engagement. At my work, it's expecting that you give a student an opportunity to catch up on missed tutorials and contact them so that we can work something out together. So, for me, the reciprocal relationships value is that something positive will come out of it if I give something and they respond back to what I've offered.

An aspect of reciprocal relationships in my classroom is my borrow policy. I have lots of spare rulers, pens, and equipment—because often, particularly with Pacific girls and I know it is sad to say—sometimes they just turn up without what they need. My borrow policy is that they have to give me something of theirs in exchange for something that they need and at the end of the lesson we give things back to one another.

Teachers can build reciprocal relationships in the standard learner progress interviews, and in the multicultural days, or when you have other big celebrations in the schools. It's always good then to pounce on some parents and look at what skills they have to offer—like it might be making panikeke. Grab them, bring them in. I say to them, "You know, we've got a few kids here whose passion is baking. Could you come in and show how you make those?", or "You know about luau. It would be good for you to come in and show them that this is a Samoan delicacy, and this is how you make it." I like to invite them to utilise their talents and knowledge with our children. Or if they're the elders who are into weaving, they can come in and share.

### Example in practice: Drawing on expertise

In one school we visited, with New Zealand European learners the minority, teachers tap on the parents' shoulders asking them to come in and share what they know. The teachers there embrace Samoan language and culture because they're the biggest part of the school's makeup. Reciprocal relationships are not left to the Samoan teacher. The school has built a Samoan language nest where only Samoan is spoken. Those kids are going into classes and being the Samoan language teachers—teaching pronunciation of A E I O U and simple phrases. In syndicate meetings, teachers are asked, "Have you tried contacting so and so's granddad to come in?", or "Have you done a follow-on lesson from the language nest children's visit?", "How have you shown your class that learning about Samoan is not limited to the language nest?" Teachers list their Pasifika parents and learn about parents' knowledge and skills that could be offered to their class.

Respect, family, service, belonging, and leadership also feature in this example.

## *What is the responsibility of educators in terms of the reciprocal relationships value?*

Educators sit in a position of power. We need to understand that and look at how we make sure as much as possible that there is an equal power for learners, rather than thinking my own way is the right way. Our responsibility is ensuring that we know what our learners' languages are, what their cultural values and practices are, what their parents would like us to foster with their child—having a strong understanding of these before launching into developing a programme.

A lot of the times when I'm working with students, especially with our Pasifika students, I am direct and say, "I'm going to give you this extra time to do your work and I expect that you will reciprocate by doing it by that deadline." However, I want them to do the work because they feel it's important rather than because they know that I want it, and I'm working on that. I find sometimes my Pacific students want more direction than other students, just to know they are on the right track. I want to make sure they realise I want them to be confident to do the thinking.

I scan the room and if I see students by themselves, I whisper to the tutors about that so they can connect with them. That allows students to sit by themselves if they want to, but still be connected, but we also encourage them to move to go and sit with another student. I try to foster reciprocal relationships in my lecturing, which helps with other values of belonging and inclusion. We've also really made the assignments connect tightly with reciprocal relationships. In one assignment they choose one of the lecture topics and unpack it through a performance or presentation. Because of the focus on relationships in the course, they ask each other a lot of questions and share ideas well, which is good.

I give examples of my upbringing and life and history to help students understand Pacific values—like for reciprocal relationships I explain that my father is a leader of the family, and that he'll support somebody with money or with food and that he doesn't expect anything in return. It's not a loan, but at a certain point in time one of our father's children might be the recipient of his recipient's family doing something for us. We have a very strong family resemblance. I went to a conference in Hawaii and to church there, and people asked, "Are you related to …? You look just like him." When they found out I was, they wanted to give me lunch—they pulled out some money and pressed it into my hand and then ran away before I had the chance to say no. So, I'm holding a crispy $50 note for getting my lunch. As a Pacific person, I know this is because way back in the day, my parents did something for them that they valued. So, years later, when they didn't have the privilege of giving back to my parents,

I'm the recipient of something quite generous that wasn't from me doing something, but from my parents. That's an example of reciprocal relationships in practice—there is an obligation and there's a gifting of support from this. There is an enormous feeling of obligation and it may not be paid in kind, but you don't just sit back and ignore it. I explain things like this to help my students to understand that for some Pacific families, this reciprocity plays out in putting together money for others and for going to a funeral and so on. Those sorts of actions, that's the values in action. When I share stories that help explain the values, I often see how the Pacific students look afterwards, because they understand these things.

> There is an enormous feeling of obligation and it may not be paid in kind, but you don't just sit back and ignore it.

In summary, attending to the value of reciprocal relationships means knowing yourself and knowing others. It means caring for others when they are in need, giving what you can, and graciously receiving support when others see you are in need. Relationships stem from responsibility, duty, and service and everyone has responsibility for nurturing relationships. Understanding and acting in ways that respect and nurture the vā support the development of strong reciprocal relationships. Reciprocity is important, expected, and freely given.

### Discussion questions

Tasi   *How can educators use the value of reciprocal relationships to enhance the effectiveness of their work with learners and families?*

Lua   *What educator behaviours may Pacific students and families expect in relation to the value of reciprocal relationships? How might they respond if they don't experience these?*

Tolu   *What responsibilities and obligations do educators have across all aspects of the learning setting in relation to the value of reciprocal relationships?*

## Ideas for extra reading

**Nurturing relationships and honouring responsibilities: A Pacific perspective**
Thaman (2008)

Beginning and finishing with poetry, this article examines insights into what Tongan values offer in relation to relationships and learning. A key focus is on individuals and teachers attempting to understand one another through understanding the cultures that surround them and using this understanding to inform their practice.

**From good to great: The 10 habits of phenomenal educators for Pacific learners in New Zealand tertiary education**
Chu-Fuluifaga & Ikiua-Pasi (2021)

This report presents findings from teaching observations and talanoa interviews with tertiary educators and surveys with learners in a study into highly effective practice across diverse tertiary education contexts. The strengths-based approach helped identify characteristics, habits, and practices of educators who make a strong positive difference for their learners, which are described in this report.

**Caring for classroom relationality in Pasifika education: A space-based understanding**
Reynolds (2018)

This article discusses how relationships can be seen through the notion of "va"—the relational space that exists between entities and people—and "teu le va"—the care for "va" needed to reach an ideal state. "Va" is proposed as a way for the education system to rethink strategies intended to promote Pacific achievement.

**Retaining non-traditional students: Lessons learnt from Pasifika students in New Zealand**
Benseman, Coxon, Anderson, & Anae (2006)

Challenges to retention and progress in tertiary education for Pacific students including family pressure, motivation, financial pressures, and lack of support services are discussed in this article alongside possible solutions suggested by student participants. Support centred around Pacific learners' needs such as pastoral care and social and academic engagement between learners and lecturers and the institution and community are discussed as promoting learner interest in and completion of courses.

### 'Polycultural' capital and educational achievement among NZ-born Pacific peoples
Mila-Schaaf & Robinson (2010)

This article analyses Pasifika education as an intercultural event from the perspective of secondary school students. The author builds on Pacific theories about Pacific people, such as "brotherhood" groups, calls for increased teacher- and institution-based intercultural competence, and discusses potential advantages for learners of culturally distinctive social spaces. Reciprocal connections, educator characteristics, and relationships are discussed as strength-based approaches to understanding Pacific perspectives.

## References

Benseman, J., Coxon, E., Anderson, H., & Anae, M. (2006). Retaining non-traditional students: Lessons learnt from Pasifika students in New Zealand. *Higher Education Research & Development, 25*(2), 147–162. https://doi.org/10.1080/07294360600610388

Chu-Fuluifaga, C., & Ikiua-Pasi, J. (2021). *From good to great: The 10 habits of phenomenal educators for Pacific learners in New Zealand tertiary education.* Ako Aotearoa. https://ako.ac.nz/knowledge-centre/from-good-to-great-the-10-habits-of-phenomenal-educators-for-pacific-learners/

Hunter, J., Hunter, R., Bills, T., Cheung, I., Hannant, B., Kritesh, K., & Lachaiya, R. (2016). Developing equity for Pāsifika learners within a New Zealand context: Attending to culture and values. *New Zealand Journal of Educational Studies, 51*(2), 197–209. https://doi.org/10.1007/s40841-016-0059-7

Mila-Schaaf, K., & Robinson, E. (2010). 'Polycultural' capital and educational achievement among NZ-born Pacific peoples. *Mai Review, 1*, 1–18. http://www.review.mai.ac.nz/mrindex/MR/article/download/307/307-2282-1-PB.pdf

Reynolds, M. (2018). Caring for classroom relationality in Pasifika education: A space-based understanding. *Waikato Journal of Education, 23*(1), 71–84. https://doi.org/10.15663/wje.v23i1.575

Thaman, K. H. (2008). Nurturing relationships and honouring responsibilities: A Pacific perspective. *International Review of Education, 54*, 459–473. https://doi.org/10.1007/s11159-008-9092-1

**Educator practice—Demonstrating and nurturing reciprocal relationships**

For most chapters in this book, a table of practice implications has been provided using ideas from messages within the educator voices. Here, we provide some insights from the chapter and invite you to create, use, and revisit lists of practice implications and possibilities for yourself, with your team, and across your institution. We encourage rereading of the educator voices and having discussions with Pacific learners, families, and colleagues to assist.

Give freely without expecting anything in return. Encourage learners and show belief in their capability to succeed. Encourage co-operation and community building. Support learners to collaborate with each other and feel comfortable seeking assistance from educators. Support learners to rely on each other as well as on educators. Help learners see themselves as capable and confident in their curriculum area/s. Devote time to discussion and relationship building. Encourage learners to discuss and work in differing social groups to build relationships and foster fa'aaloalo.

Respect and incorporate the languages and cultures of learners in your practice. Seek to understand each individual learner's skills and interests and share yours with them. Have the learning community find out what each other does and achieves outside of the learning context. Find out how learners can be supported.

Ask parents what values they foster in their child and would like the learning context to support. Share stories of reciprocal relationships in Pacific communities. Share your own experiences of what goes around, comes around and ask students to share their stories.

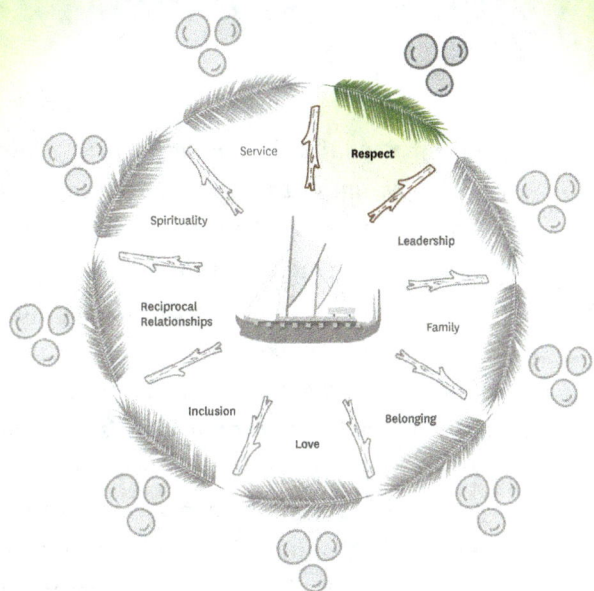

Chapter Eight

# Respect

**What does respect mean to Pacific people? How can learning environments strongly demonstrate and nurture Pacific perspectives of respect?**

> *Ehara ahau i te rangatira, engari he ata ahau nō te tangata.*
> *I am not a chiefly person, but rather the reflection of one.*
> *(Whakataukī 76, p. 22, Ngā Pēpeha a ngā Tipuna)*

In Māori (and Pacific) worldviews, respect is connected to manaakitanga, translated as kindness or generosity. Manaakitanga comprises three words: "mana" (supernatural authority, power, or charisma); "aki" (to encourage or exhort); "tanga" (a relay of people). Manaakitanga, then, is our innate power to encourage others' inherent mana, or to embody respect. We enact respect or mana-enhancing behaviours by recognising that mana is not of ourselves but is inherited from those preceding us. We reflect the mana of Te Atua/God and of tūpuna/ancestors. A well-known Pacific leader once stated, "the way up is down". Respect is kindled as we walk in humility, recognising others' familial mana. Tamariki reflect the mana of their tūpuna. "Tamariki", although translated as "children" in English, links with the Māori name for the sun, "Tamanuiterā", and with "ariki", literally meaning, "small sparks of chiefly, imprinted light" (Tapiata, 2018). Tamariki carry the mana and reflection of their rangatira/chiefly whakapapa. Respect their mana through manaakitanga.

We are very grateful to Dr Rae Si'ilata (Ngāti Raukawa/Tūhourangi/Fiji, with whānau connections to Samoa, Tonga, and Tokelau), Director of Va'atele Education Consulting and Senior Lecturer at Te Whare Wānanga o Awanuiārangi for this contribution about respect. Vinaka.

- Respect is fundamentally important to Pacific people.
- Empathy, humility, and openness are important components of respectful behaviour and interactions.
- Understanding how Pacific learners show respect and demonstrating respect through teaching is important for ensuring teaching can maximise learning.
- Respect includes respect for elders, their knowledge, and contributions and respect for people with important roles or qualifications.
- Knowing and using Pacific language words, phrases, proverbs, and songs can help demonstrate respect for Pacific people.

Being respectful and feeling respected are key to strong relationships. Respect requires knowledge, understanding, acknowledgement, and giving time to others. Through respectful relationships and finding out about their Pacific learners' ways of viewing the world, educators can learn about their learners' individual identities and priorities (Samu, 2006). Such teacher understandings help teachers develop a rich idea of the Pacific learner as a whole person (Samu, 2006). Mutual respect can develop through learner–educator interactions, particularly if educators are attuned to learners bringing experiences and ways of communicating to the relationship that may differ from the educator's (Tuioti, 2002). Educators must demonstrate respect for their learners as individuals and as learners, and challenge and suitably scaffold each learner's learning (Spiller, 2012). Respect is shown to Pacific learners and their families through ensuring they know that their values and aspirations are important in the learning setting and ensuring they feel a strong sense of belonging there (Airini et al., 2010).

Let's hear from our Pacific educators …

## *What does respect mean to you?*

Respect is acknowledging one another. It is about active listening. Respect is a two-way thing, not just me demanding respect from my students—I have to demonstrate it as well in order to get respect. Coming from a Samoan family, respect was instilled in us from birth. It is about knowing your place and respecting that relational space between you and another person. Sometimes it is unspoken, and it is just intuitive, you just know—particularly in the Pacific space. Respect is about what is conveyed and what is expected in terms of respect.

Respect involves empathy and looking at things from the other person's perspective and recognising what they bring to the relationship. Respect involves knowing that there are a lot of values and a lot of practices that children from a different culture bring with them that we need to consider in building a relationship with them. Respect plays out in mutual understanding that each person brings a wealth of knowledge, strengths, and skills themselves and from their community to their relationships. It is having the knowledge that we each learn a lot from one another and being open to that learning. Humility is an important part of respect, to acknowledge that we are all learners from one another.

When I came to university to learn my Cook Island language—because I hadn't been taught by my mother—I asked the lecturer why we are losing our language. He said that, from the Cook Island perspective, when you're in another country, particularly a host country, it's good manners and respectful to use the language of our hosts. So, the value of respect that has been ingrained in us has been at our expense, because we've lost our language. We defer to English because that's the language of our host community. Things have changed now, but for a long time, using the language of those you were with was seen as the respectful thing to do. That's one example that shows how Pacific people consider respect.

Thank you for the question. Going back to my Tokelauan culture, respect to me is about respecting your elders and people who are older than you.

Back home we respect old people because of their mana. Here in New Zealand, I can see respect for elders is really strong with our Tokelau community. At any gathering, if there's elders there, you don't really talk—the elders are given the opportunity to talk and they speak on behalf of everyone. It's how I was brought up and in my earlier years in Samoa. You give respect to the elders whether they know things or not. You give the respect to the authority of people who are older than you. You look after them, whether you are related to them or not—you know it comes back to being part of the community.

Respect is really important. I grew up in Samoa and we especially respect our older people—they are the role models for us. The model we use in Samoa is that if you respect one person, it will come back to you. You have to respect other people, respect your parents, and then when you go to the village and when you go to the other families, we always show respect to be a good role model. That's the main thing I learnt from my parents. If anything happened in the village, we have to contribute—we don't think about the money or the bank because we alofa to everyone. We're there at a funeral or a wedding or whatever—everyone contributes, which is a part of respecting and loving other people—this is the way we do things and our kids grow up and see us doing that.

Respect is a deep one. Respect is putting yourself last. It's connected to family. When I came to New Zealand and I didn't know how to speak English, respect was not talking until I was spoken to or specifically asked a question, and then I knew that I was open to discuss something. Even when I started university, I showed respect by not talking very much; I was just quiet and did what I was told. That was a lot of my upbringing—doing as I was told.

*Things that you do show your respect.*

I was brought up in Fiji, so I think respect is really important. It shows how much value you place in that person by how you show respect. Things that you do show your respect. You go into a house; you take your shoes off. In a Fijian sense, we always go in through the back door, not the front door, because that's not for family. You go through the back door and you come through, take your shoes off, and sit on the floor, so you're always at the bottom and everyone else is more elevated than you are. Respect is keeping your thoughts to yourself and always taking time to mull things over rather than what could be termed as a confrontational approach, like speaking straight away. Instead, you just say to yourself, "Ok, I will go and think about that." You always try and find angles of how the other person is seeing things, which is sometimes counter to how we learn at university. I have been trying to explain to my daughter that, even though my Mum has Alzheimer's, we still have to show her respect. We treat her as we would like to be treated. So, it's a very hard thing to try and articulate but respect is that most of the time, you are the last person that you think of. You focus on how is everyone else feeling, seeing things, and working out what can I do to make them feel better or feel comfortable, and I won't necessarily speak up much unless I have thought about it very deeply and there is something to say.

Respect is about who I am. It's how I've been taught. You don't speak when older people speak. You don't say your opinion; you're not allowed to say it. I think we are like this. Coming to New Zealand from back home, this different way of learning and life is about talking and not being shy. Our respect is why we're like this—why we're so shy to speak up to say what we think. We know what we think but we are too shy to say it.

From my perspective as a Tokelauan teacher, as staff, we work as a team. We totally respect each other. We work hard but we also have fun and enjoy ourselves. Having a good time, having fun builds respect as well—it helps everyone to be confident and sociable with the parents and whoever comes in.

In a Samoan sense, if you have a title—and my title is now Dr since my PhD—respect changes relationships and expectations a bit. There are times when I'd be at community events and I'll be in the kitchen, and they'll be like, "Go sit down", but I've never been like that, and I never go out. I don't go, "Hello, my name is Dr …", because in the community they know who I am, and they know there's a title there, so they try to shove me out of the everyday work I used to be involved in. That's the community showing their service and respect to people with titles. Even here, some of the students know that I have that title and some of them will address me in that way, especially if they're Samoan students. They'll come and they'll "talofa", even if they're New Zealand born. I tell them that's not necessary here, but because they've probably been brought up that way. There are a couple of boys who still act like that today—they give me a little thank you, but it was never eye-to-eye. Sometimes the title blocks the idea of relationships that I've been trying to build in the classroom. They are aware there is that space that they won't cross that's part of their upbringing. I'm fine with accepting the acknowledgement, but I don't encourage it. It is the way of showing respect, but I just feel like an everyday person.

### What can respect look like in learning settings?

Once my students walk through the door, I show my respect for them by presenting a nice smiling face and make them feel welcome and acknowledged. I greet them and, if I have latecomers, I wouldn't make a big deal of it. I have a routine where I have a late notebook by the door for them to write in the time they arrive and the reason they're late, and then they just join the class without any disruptions. I don't ask them why they are late and be all pissy about it. Then once I have finished doing what I was doing at the time, I go and acknowledge them and greet them and ask how they are and then kind of warm up to saying, "Have you written in the book? Have you explained why you were late?" The kids are really good, they just tell you anyway straight away. They know they were late and being late is a sign of disrespect to them, and they try to avoid that at all costs.

In the learning setting, educators can encourage all their learners to understand and use respectful words and gestures, like if they're having lunch, teaching them not to reach in front of others, but to go purposely around or behind. That would be like "Wow" for the Pasifika children, because what they do at home and their cultural values would be demonstrated and nurtured in the learning environment. That would add a bit more to that feeling of belonging in this place for them and they'd know there is an understanding that what they do at home and in the learning setting are not too separate. I'm sure the parents would be touched as well. This just opens up and demonstrates more understanding about how they feel and what they prioritise. Because when you see something that you feel is disrespectful, the teacher might not know that that's a disrespectful thing—but when they see something is causing an unhappy feeling, it's good if they go home and think about it and work out how to change things, rather than asking for answers straight away. Educators need to ask their class, "If there is something I do or some of us do that's not in line with your understanding of respect, then let me know."

Respect is about knowing the learners well enough to know what their strengths and skills are, what they are good at, what they love doing, what resonates with them. At the end of the day, whatever their background, respect is teachers accepting children for who they are and feeling what an opportunity they have, to have these children in their classroom—what a great privilege it is.

Respect is looking out for each other—seeing if you need something and giving it to you if it is something I can give. If teachers can be a little bit more giving, like even like sharing food, always making sure they have some food, and sharing it and inviting parents in and providing food. The whole thing of sharing together shows respect and it shows that I want to learn from you.

### Example in practice: Learning mathematics

Respect was shown to learners in many ways in this mathematics lesson on multiplying and dividing integers and revision of calculating GST inclusive and exclusive prices. The teacher greeted all students by name at the door as they arrived, "Hi girls! How are you?" She made personal links with those she knows from her community. Learning intentions, the lesson starter activity and new learning was written in full sentences on the board and students were asked to identify words they didn't know. She checked everyone could see the board and was comfortable. She asked learners to respect the new fans and mini whiteboards in the classroom which she purchased to improve their learning conditions, and one said, "You really care about us." She warned them about what was coming in the lesson and when she would be asking for volunteers. When students were whispering off topic, she whispered to them, "What are you whispering about?" For the game, she organised the groups using a line up—asking everyone to line up in alphabetical order according to their favourite food. Through this they all learnt something new about one another. In the group game, more capable learners supported those less capable. As it was a double lesson, there was a walking break in the middle for students to go outside, managed by the learners. The teacher asked learners about their out-of-school activities, responsibilities, and fundraising. She linked new learning to contexts relevant to them related to these. Students were keen to take opportunities to write their answers on the whiteboard. She checked for readiness when moving on in the lesson activities and moved down to desk level when helping one-to-one. She reminded learners of useful prior learning and set high expectations, "Do as much as you can." Students were used to helping one another and asking each other for help. When, during the lesson, a ball flew through the glass window, she remained calm, sent for the caretaker, checked everyone was all right, and used humour to calm the class: "Well, at least we're getting some fresh air." Students took initiative to help. She asked students to make a number-based poster for her which explains about themselves for homework.

Again, many values were present in this lesson including respect, service, leadership, and family.

> *It warms my heart when you see a non-Pacific or even another Pacific person showing respect in a Pacific way, like not walking or reaching in front of someone.*

For educators, it is important to understanding what respect means for each student. I have been in a class where I saw a teacher patting someone's head, and I felt, "Oh no, that's tapu." It warms my heart when you see a non-Pacific or even another Pacific person showing respect in a Pacific way, like not walking or reaching in front of someone. I was in a café once and a guy came behind me to grab a serviette and he just said, "Tulou, oh excuse me" and I was like, "Oh, that's so good." So, educators understanding and using words and gestures to show respect means a lot. It means that they understand that it's not just a word, it's how you show it that's important. Lecturers do it here where I've had like a tangi and they have been so kind around that. By educators demonstrating that kind of understanding around respect, you just know that that teacher understands what is valuable to me.

Pacific people really respect each person for who they are. They know who each person is, and their connections and they look after one another. For example, a Pacific cohort of teachers upgrading their qualifications worked together in wonderful ways—a really good model for how I would love all of our students to work. They shared ideas and brought food to share each day, and there was the hierarchy—they knew that the minister's wife was the one who would say the lotu or the prayer at the beginning of the day. They had a shared understanding of the protocols, and they were all very good at delivering their presentations orally and singing and other important aspects of culture.

### How can teachers demonstrate the value of respect in their teaching?

Respect in the home sense carries through into my work. Respect is very much one of those traditional Samoan values we were brought up with—we listened to our parents; we knew what to do in extended family events. My Mum would teach us, saying, "I saw you doing that. Why were you doing that?" There was never a telling off, unless it was something major, and that's how I've taught children about behaviour as a classroom teacher as well.

As a child in New Zealand classrooms, I knew the teacher was somebody who I had to show much respect for, by listening and by watching. I've never followed that practice you hear about of never looking a teacher eye to eye because it shows disrespect, because we were told showing respect was always about listening, and that you listen by looking face to face, and that's how I've always done it. For me, showing respect was having a closeness between myself and a teacher for communicating—I wouldn't sit at the back and put my hand up, "I know the answer." I preferred the space to be closer between myself and teacher when I spoke with them, and that's how I've done it. As a lecturer, I've always used that proximity idea as a way of showing respect towards my students—I approach them to have a conversation just between myself and the student, and I've never had any experience where a student has backed off. I just feel that if I'm having a conversation about something to do with them, I'd rather talk just with them and not yell it out. Even when I'm in class, and I know that there's a student in my class who I know has something they can share, I will always approach them first, to say, "Hey, I was wondering if you'd take part." For me, that's showing respect for my students. I always hope that that's how they see me; that in the way that I approach them I show respect towards them as an individual and as a learner. I want them to rely on being able to come to me and talk to me or question me because of my manner of approaching them. That's how I've always seen respect from how we were brought up.

Teachers can demonstrate respect in their teaching by working one on one. When they talk, talk, talk to the whole group, for some of our Tokelauan children, it can be hard to pick up words that are important and some of the words we don't understand. So respectful teaching would be really breaking learning down into understandable concepts and connecting with children, rather than just standing up front of the class. If the teacher just talk, talk, talks, I would never say anything because I don't understand. Even after school I won't ask, because I don't want to feel I'm a burden to the teacher.

Teachers demonstrate respect by showing they really want to ensure that learners retain a strong sense of identity and their language and cultural practices. Bringing the community in and going out to the community is something that we need to strengthen in education. Teachers can model and encourage everyone to be involved in language learning, especially in the language weeks—they can learn and use phrases from the Niue language, and when they're talking to parents they can use simple phrases of their language, and at least greet them in their language. Teachers can make sure they give opportunities for developing skills important to Pacific people that sit within our curriculum, like recall, memory, and helping children prepare and give oral presentations—all skills that are really important for Pacific people. This kind of teaching shows respect by showing that the teacher acknowledges these languages, cultural practices, and skills as important parts of who we are. This is so important because, once you lose your language and skills, a lot of the cultural background is lost as well.

If you show respect by speaking with the kids, they will follow you. Respect is in the way we approach and talk with them and the parents. Even though it might be about something we saw that is not appropriate—we have to find out ways to approach the parents about it, and we have to make sure they feel welcome and we have to listen to their point of view, and respect the kids' point of view. Showing respect is also showing the kids how we feel. It's really important so that they can understand why you're frustrated and grumpy, like saying, "I'm grumpy because you are not listening to me", or "I'm telling you that there seems to be no one helping me—I need some help in this job." You have to be honest and share your feelings and the way you do things.

I deliberately arrange my tables in groups rather than in single file—it shows that we are all in this together, we are all there to support one another. I have quick quizzes at the beginning of the lesson to reinforce the learning from the previous lesson and I have random strategies to involve them in answering. I will ask maybe the girl with the longest hair can answer this question, or the girl who lives the closest to the school, which shows them that it could be anybody who's chosen and I am not just picking on certain people. I don't like to put them on the spot, so I give them warning beforehand that I'll be asking them, and if they don't feel comfortable, then they can nominate someone from their table.

### Can educator knowledge about Pacific communities help them demonstrate respect?

Yes. We don't ask and we don't question—we listen and we do. When we do speak, it's limited. We do what we're told. They're the rules that we live our lives by that teach us to be humble. We know that one day our time will come and then we will expect our children to listen to us. In the New Zealand culture, though, it's different now with our children. We tell them how

> *We don't ask and we don't question—we listen and we do.*

to respect but we don't have the balance between respect and speaking up. We want them not to be afraid to talk out and share what they need to get out there because that helps them in the education system if they speak up—they're more likely to get help and that's how we've tried to move—more into a Western way of thinking. But if teachers understand that to be respectful for our Pacific learners is not to speak up and not to question, then maybe they can look at respect from another cultural perspective and change some of their ways of teaching in response. Not all teachers realise that, if the learner never talks in the class, they're showing the teacher their respect—it's not that they don't know or can't answer. Teachers can show respect for their learners in understanding this view of respect and accommodating it in their teaching.

I tell my student teachers, "If you have a chance go and live in another culture, go and immerse yourself in another way of life, because that will give you insight and practical experience to develop understanding of others." It's very easy to read about things in a book and the principles of teaching, but until you've had that lived experience it's not as easy to make respectful connections. When you've had experience in Pacific communities, you can draw from these in interactions, like saying, "When I was living there …", or "When I visited there, I could see that this is what they were doing …" which helps build connections with others. It's not always practicable to experience Pacific communities, but even within our communities here in Aotearoa, teachers can find out when festivals and other events are happening and find ways to support these and build them into their teaching. For example, this week is Niue language week, and I wonder how many teachers are going to go out into a language nest to find out what they're like. I wonder what teachers are doing to support our Pacific culture and our languages. Teachers could easily write all the language weeks on the calendar plan and be doing something with their students around these. They could plan a trip out to the community or invite our elders in. There needs to be a lot more of that happening so we can all understand each other a bit more—those activities build mutual respect because the community will feel valued and that their children are going to be able to retain their sense of identity and be proud of it.

When we did some diversity research a few years ago, the biggest concern for Pacific families with children going from early childhood learning language nest into school was for the school to have a Pacific teacher, because even if that teacher wasn't in the new entrants' classroom, there would be a teacher within that school their child would have a connection with. Pacific teachers are also often a go-between, for the school and the parents, someone parents feel comfortable with. Without a Pacific teacher at the school, many Pacific parents feel a huge gap, and might travel to another school further away, because they know they have a Samoan teacher, for example. If there's a Pacific teacher, parents know there is someone at the school who is going to support their Pacific language and culture and promote them within the school. Sadly, for some children leaving language nests, when they get to school there is nothing supporting their language or culture. So, all teachers considering what others bring to the school, the wealth of knowledge, skills, and cultural practices and tapping into that helps show a huge amount of respect. A lot of our knowledge is passed down orally, and so some of our old people have a lot of knowledge, and that's how they were taught. They may not have formal qualifications, but they're the ones who have the authentic cultural knowledge and understanding—so teachers making space for them to come and provide that knowledge shows respect. I don't think that happens enough.

### *Is there knowledge other than cultural knowledge that would help teachers feel and demonstrate respect?*

Pacific people encounter racist situations on a daily basis. When teachers know more about Pacific communities and are aware of those situations, they can help to address the racism. It is starting—in the weekend, there was an issue on the news of Māori and Pacific babies not getting the same opportunities for resuscitation as European babies—it didn't surprise me because people make assumptions. For example, I don't overtly look Pacific and when my daughter was born the nurses made an assumption that I was Pālagi or Papa'ā. Then my mother and my sister who are both very Polynesian looking arrived and when they left the nurse came to give my daughter an injection for tuberculosis, saying they do that routinely for Pacific babies. I thought this race-based practice makes a huge assumption. My sister told me all of her babies had the injection and she didn't know she could question it. She didn't know that the European babies weren't given it, and we felt assumptions were being made about our lifestyle and that we were not being treated respectfully. There are incidents like this that happen all the time, like covert racism. So, if teachers can see things through Pacific eyes a little more and understand that we do have a lot to grapple with in this society, which isn't always geared towards Pacific people, this can help with them demonstrating respect.

We have got very traditional ways of interacting with parents at our school. We use a very traditional school way of having all the desks out in the hall and 5 minutes to talk with each parent. I think, "How does that fit with the school's values or with Pasifika values in terms of respect?" It is taken as the way we do things, but is there a critique of those kinds of practices in terms of the values of the school? You don't get enough time; it is not enough time. By the time you have introduced yourself, it is time to go. But now we split them up into departments rather than all being together in the hall, so if you get a challenging parent, you have your HOD assistant and your HOD in the same room to jump in if they need to. Teachers having and using Pacific understandings of respect could help make our parent–teacher meetings more appropriate.

*Do you use contexts that relate to the Pacific in your teaching?*

Yes, most definitely—using Pacific contexts really helps Pacific learners feel legitimised and validated in the class. Their eyes light up and I find them more engaged when I do that.

*How can educators foster and develop the value of respect?*

In our Tongan immersion class, to develop understanding of respect, I ask the children to go and talk with their parents about faka'apa'apa (respect) and they come back with the different views of their parents and their grandparents. Then I put all of what they have found out together. I also emphasise good behaviour, "Any good behaviour you do, that's respect. When you listen to your teacher, that's respect. When you just walk past somebody and you say the word tulou (excuse me), that's respect." That's what I tell them—that all of the good behaviours show respect. That's a main theme in the values I work on with them. When they understand that, they learn about humility and loyalty, because everything hinges on respect. If you have good behaviour, you don't get in trouble. If you've got good behaviour, the teacher doesn't have to keep stopping. When we have good discipline, kids have good learning. It's hard to apply that kind of teaching with children of other cultures and that's why I'm happy to have the Tongan class now. I have good communication with the parents. I talk straight to the parents so if something happens inside the classroom, I can approach the parents about it.

To me, respect is first and foremost about relationships and it builds from there. What's really helped me in my teaching is respecting children by getting to know them and them also getting to know me. They like to know my background because then they can find some common ground where they can just ask anything. I tell them that, "I know I have to earn your respect, and you have to earn mine. Actually, you already have my respect and you don't want to lose my respect." I always start off with that and I've found it useful especially with some of the more challenging students. They know more about what to expect. The values that we're trying to teach them here are the values that they have in their own homes. They come from those backgrounds. They go to church on Sundays. They know that they need to be respectful in a chapel setting or wherever. The same applies here at school. I think because I know that I have an advantage because I've grown up the same way. But every educator should understand about respect for their Pasifika children and families.

> *respect is first and foremost about relationships and it builds from there*

Pasifika students will come with a deep sense and understanding of respect, but there might be other students in the classroom who don't have the same depth of understanding of respect. I think a good way is to demonstrate respect yourself as a teacher—model what we expect, promote respect as very important, as part of your teaching. Then students will get a sense of understanding and see these ways of being as normal. Teachers can look to their own backgrounds—Scottish, or English, or Irish—and make sure they have a strong understanding of their own identity, while knowing they don't have to lose sight of who they are to demonstrate the Pacific perspectives of respect. Them knowing that we're here, we're part of the Pacific, and being in this nation is about encountering Pacific values that are really important for Pacific people, that they can also take on and add to who they are and how they view themselves. If teachers look to where their own families came from, they can see that there may be connections that aren't very different from Pacific views. Looking at what we all share can be powerful for building relationships and respecting one another's perspectives.

I help the students respect one another by getting them to move around a lot and work with different people in the class, especially in the first few weeks. I do a lot of moving around them as well, so by the end of those weeks they've moved around to every corner of the lecture theatre. They've mingled, they've talked. I spend time in my class building in interactive activities so they learn about each other's names and other things that can help build relationships and respect in class. This makes it a safer environment for everyone, which is really important because of the content we cover. I want them all to be happy to share. The evidence of that working is that they talk and bring things up and debate ideas and they come and see me about them.

I nurture respect by referring back to our school values. I don't ask learners why they are doing what they are doing—I ask instead for them to reflect on their actions and whether they fit in with the school values. Our school values are based on the Māori values, so they fit quite nicely with the Pacific values. Our students understand our school values, because from Year 9 we have a good way of training them and developing that knowledge. But they don't have the same understanding as one another of the Pasifika values. Pasifika interpretations of the values aren't seen so much in our school's learning environments—but they are seen in other places, like in our school Pasifika contexts like the "Poly group" and "Big Sister" where the girls act in ways they all know to be appropriate.

Universities have not caught up with how they should treat us when we do cultural labour. Culturally, I work to support the institution and the students. It's not measured or acknowledged. I feel disrespected and sometimes I feel they're taking advantage of me because of the way I work and my values. Cultural labour encompasses giving back to our research participants in ways that fit with our cultural values of service and reciprocity. These contributions take time away from being able to do things our institution requires. Our experience is needed for many initiatives, such as to inform the management plan, set up an advisory group, make suggestions, and practically help with a fono. We wouldn't be able to hold our heads up in the Pacific community if we didn't make these contributions; however, the lack of recognition of what we bring and do in our institutions reduces our sense of belonging in these places, and if we're not feeling a strong sense of belonging, how can we help instil this in our Pacific learners or demonstrate suitable practice for our learners? As a consequence of the time and energy used in cultural labour, we don't climb up the ladder as much as others and that's to our and our families' detriment. We're not doing enough of the "right things" because our values, which help make us cultural assets to our institutions, are based on other things. Having more educators with culturally based understandings and pushing for change is needed for us to feel our contributions and expertise are respected by our colleagues and institutions.

Sometimes, I feel disrespected by my institution because of required processes and expectations. For example, we used to have a system where extensions were approved by somebody else, not the lecturer. Students would get told, "You don't have paperwork for this extension." We don't have that system any more, which is just as well. Our institutions need to modify processes like this, so they are fit for the students they serve. They need to figure out innovative, creative ways to help students.

In summary, attending to the value of respect means acknowledging that each person holds the mana of their forebears and showing respect for elders and authority. It is attending to the relational space between people. Respect is acknowledging the breadth of knowledge and experience that each person brings. It is listening, showing empathy, and putting others first. Respect is using cultural protocols and understanding culturally linked behaviour. Respect is shown in words, body language, and actions. Respect is showing kindness, manaakitanga, and generosity.

### Discussion questions
Tahi   *What can the value of respect encompass for Pacific people?*
Rua   *How can respect be demonstrated and nurtured by educators?*

Toru  *How can educators demonstrate respect for Pacific priorities, languages, and cultural activities in their interactions and teaching?*

**Ideas for extra reading**
Raising the achievement of priority learners in primary school
McKenzie (2018)

This article explores achievement of Pacific students in Aotearoa primary schools along with the values and perspectives of participant teachers and students. The importance for school learning of engagement in early childhood education and positive relationships built through "respect" are discussed as pivotal for engagement in learning.

"In order to teach you, I must know you." The Pasifika initiative: A professional development project for teachers
Allen, Taleni, & Robertson (2008)

The study involved early childhood to secondary educators travelling to Samoa for 10 days to explore how Pacific learners learn and how they can implement these ways into their own practice. Prior to travel, the educators learnt about the Samoan language and culture. A vital value for this work highlighted by educators is respect.

"How can we teach them when they won't listen?": How teacher beliefs about Pasifika values and Pasifika ways of learning affect student behaviour and achievement
Spiller (2012)

Respect was discussed by learners and the educators in this study. The article highlights the potential for educators and Pacific students to misunderstand each other and their roles. Educator understanding and being respectful are discussed as pivotal to catering well for Pacific learners.

R*E*S*P*E*C*T: A value vital for Pasifika learners
Rimoni & Averill (2019)

This article articulates notions around respect as perceived and implemented by Pacific and non-Pacific educators, showing that deeper understanding of the Pacific value is needed by our non-Pacific teachers to effectively teach Pacific learners.

## References

Airini, Anae, M., Mila-Schaaf, K., with Coxon, E., Mara, D., & Sanga, K. (2010). *Teu le va: Relationships across research and policy: A collective approach to knowledge generation and policy development for action towards Pasifika education success*. Ministry of Education. https://www.educationcounts.govt.nz/publications/pacific/teu-le-va-relationships-across-research-and-policy-in-pasifika-education

Allen, P., Taleni, L. I. E. T., & Robertson, J. (2009). 'In order to teach you, I must know you': The Pasifika initiative: A professional development project for teachers. *New Zealand Journal of Educational Studies, 44*(2), 47–62.

Mead, H. M., & Grove, N. (2004). *Ngā Pēpeha a ngā Tīpuna*. Victoria University Press.

McKenzie, A. (2018). *Raising the achievement of priority learners in primary schools*. Doctoral dissertation, Auckland University of Technology.

Rimoni, F., & Averill, R. (2019). Respect: A value vital for Pasifika learners. *Set: Research Information for Teachers*, (3), 3–11. https://doi.org/10.18296/set.0096

Samu, T. W. (2006). The 'Pasifika umbrella' and quality teaching: Understanding and responding to the diverse realities within. *Waikato Journal of Education, 12*, 35–49. https://doi.org/10.15663/wje.v12i1.297

Spiller, L. (2012). "How can we teach them when they won't listen?": How teacher beliefs about Pasifika values and Pasifika ways of learning affect student behaviour and achievement. *Set: Research Information for Teachers*, (3), 58–66. https://doi.org/10.18296/set.0393

Tapiata, H. (2018). *The value of te reo Māori*. https://www.youtube.com/watch?v=AXxXC3oVYuk

Tuioti, L. (2002). Pacific education in Aotearoa. In F. Pene, 'A. M. Taufe'ulungaki, & C. Benson (Eds.), *Tree of opportunity: Re-thinking Pacific education* (pp. 133–137). University of the South Pacific Institute of Education.

## Educator practice—Demonstrating and nurturing respect

For most chapters in this book, a table of practice implications has been provided using ideas from messages within the educator voices. Here, we provide some insights from the chapter and invite you to create, use, and revisit lists of practice implications and possibilities for yourself, with your team, and across your institution. We encourage rereading of the educator voices and having discussions with Pacific learners, families, and colleagues to assist.

Think about what respect looks like and feels like and how this value needs to be modelled and fostered. Be respectful in all actions and communication. Nurture respectful, positive educator–learner relationships and interactions. Use the mindset that learners and teachers learn from each other and that each person contributes to the community of learners through their unique blend of knowledge, strengths, and skills. Encourage everyone to see the learning context as a community respecting all members for their varied contributions.

For our Pacific students, respect is given to the elderly and to those older than themselves. Parents and elders are role models. Children in Pacific communities grow up knowing that community members support and respect one another. Acknowledge and draw from such practices of respect.

Co-create classroom expectations. Encourage students to respect one another and work together for common goals. Look for all ways that learners demonstrate engagement and respect including through their body language. Show respect for learners by understanding that they may not speak out or question unless invited and are showing their respect by waiting for an invitation to contribute.

Set aside time for positive one-on-one discussions during learning or breaks.

Share with learners how you feel and why and invite learners to reciprocate.

Demonstrate respect for Pacific colleagues, students, and families by learning and using greetings in their languages and learning about life in their communities. Understand that many Pacific educators undertake much cultural labour, support them in their work, and help develop understanding in the institution's leadership about cultural labour and its effects on individuals.

Find out about local festivals and events and incorporate ideas from these in planning and teaching. If possible, be part of learners' Pacific communities and travel to Pacific nations to better understand traditions and lifestyles. Use this learning in teaching and interactions.

Use tuakana–teina approaches in your own and peers' learning. Seek guidance from Pacific colleagues (teachers, support staff, parents …). Be open to new practices and ideas. Invite others to improve your use of language, pronunciation, and cultural understandings.

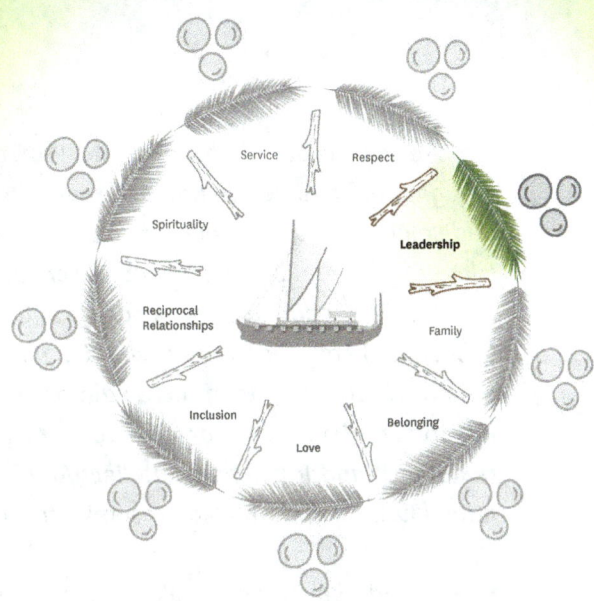

Chapter Nine

# Leadership

**What does leadership mean to Pacific people? How can learning environments utilise and embody Pacific perspectives of leadership?**

### Leadership is like the sun
#### By Kabini Sanga

Etaeta lā 'e ilifainia na sina
Na sina 'e tōdola
Na sina 'e kwanga, kwatea madakwa lā ma na unu fana tala
Nia ka fā'ago'ago, maka fāfa'alua
Nia ka tagalā na maerodo, fāfalu ka fāngasi ngasia
Gia ka lalao si'ana amoe gi nagwa fāsia na sina
   (Gula'ala language, Mala'ita, Solomon Islands)

Leadership is like the sun
Central to its community
The sun shines, giving light, providing clarity and vision
It warms, providing energy, life and renewal
It penetrates the dark, purifies undesirables and builds character
People are attracted to the sun or they hide from its glare
   (English translation)

*We are very grateful to Associate Professor Kabini Sanga for these thoughts on leadership. Kabini Sanga, MNZM, is an educator, mentor, and Solomon Islands public intellectual. Born and raised in the Solomon Islands, Kabini undertook his early schooling in his country and did all his university education overseas, first in Fiji then twice in Canada. In tribal and theocratic Mala'ita Island, Solomon Islands, he is an alafa and the principal guardian of the Gwailao tribe of East Mala'ita. He speaks, mentors, and advises in areas of leadership, ethics, education, international aid, and Indigenous intellectual traditions in the Pacific region. Kabini holds a PhD and lectures at Victoria University of Wellington.*

- Leadership is about taking responsibility, being a good role model and community member, and respecting everyone and their roles, contributions, and capabilities.
- Substantial leadership roles are given to Pacific children from an early age. There can be conflict between attending to the expectations of a leadership role and the expectations in a learning context, which can be challenging for Pacific learners and families.
- Leadership can be from the front, from the back, or beside.
- Pacific people are able to provide leadership in developing understanding of cultural knowledge, languages, and priorities.

Leadership and service are intertwined. Learning to be a good leader is a valued part of Pacific children's upbringing that can be drawn on within educational settings (Fa'ave, 2017). From a Pacific perspective, an educational leader is "an effective leader, a leader with high integrity (aloaia) and standing, who is driven by culturally responsive principles, values, aspirations and world views of the students" (Taleni et al., 2017, p. 16). Such leaders are committed to ensuring the best for all they lead, using perseverance and a humanitarian approach. Everyone takes on leadership roles in many Pacific communities, according to their knowledge, skills, age, and status. Leadership is a humble endeavour, with cultural values, family and community contribution, service and care for others, and the collective paramount (Matapo, 2017). Leadership is about contribution.

Let's hear from our Pacific educators …

*What does leadership mean to you?*

Leadership can be viewed in different ways. There might be the tau tal-atala, the talking chief who's out there representing all of the village or the community. Then there are the ones who are behind the scenes doing all of the other things and that's leadership as well. We need the spokespeople who are out there as the figureheads—people who are very charismatic and can say all the right things. That's their role, but they can't do that without all of the other supporters, and they're also leaders as well. The spokesperson will use those people to make sure that what she's saying is correct, so it's not all about being out there at the front. There's a saying about leading from behind, and for me that's really important. It's the people who are cooking, who are putting down the umu and doing the dishes and making sure that everything else is ready and going smoothly—that's also leadership. It's taking responsibility and understanding that this is a role that's important.

We have a collective way of looking at leadership. At times we do have to stand up and be an advocate, and other times we'll be content just to do things behind the scenes, because you know someone else is being the front person. It's a very fluid process, because sometimes it's really hard to be at the forefront all of the time—we have a bit of a tall poppy syndrome, that if you're going to be there at the front, you have to expect a lot of criticism; you've got to know what you're doing. Sometimes it takes a very strong person to be out there at the forefront. However, people will also say, "Well, good on you for standing up and saying what you needed to say. We respect you for doing that."

In a leadership role I have learnt a lot about respect. You have to give respect to the teachers, respect to the parents, and respect to the children and they'll respect you. When you're a leader, you respect the lower people.

> In a leadership role I have learnt a lot about respect.

My experience of the leadership role is to make things easier for others. Leadership is being a good role model. If you have good leadership, others will follow in your footsteps.

Leadership is part of serving the community and being able to support the community and especially our children. Even though I would be paid more in the English-medium centres, my goal is to lead here and promote our Samoan Pacific centre. The Ministry needs to understand that we provide a specialist service and our Pacific centres' services are so important that they really need to nurture and foster them. This is a specialist centre for language and culture and for children's identity and it should be funded appropriately. Instead, we have to cope with initiatives that interfere with things that are important to us—one of these cut across our lotu time—which is really bad. We had to explain that it's very important to us to start our day in a lotu and end our day in a lotu—this nurtures us and is very important to our culture. They don't like that; they don't like it. If they send people to visit our centre, they should be Pacific people who can speak the language of the centre and feel what we're doing here. We've had to translate things for visiting officials who don't understand.

Leadership is about you doing as you say, so what you expect from your students is what they should expect back from you. Leadership is modelling the expectations that you have, so that others follow this lead. It took me a while to learn about leadership, because being the eldest in my family I was always in a leadership role and I didn't have to work out what that meant. My parents would always involve me in discussing decisions that were made at home because I was the oldest and when my Dad passed away, leadership became a partnership between my Mum and myself. Leadership at work has a different angle because it's not my family, but the practices and the values that we learnt about leadership in the family are suitable here as well. In our view of leadership here at work, it's about everyday people, everyday roles; it's about how we want to treat everyone equally to build leadership skills.

Leadership can come in many guises. We see that in our children as well—it's when you go out of your way to help someone. Our value of giving is really important, so giving as much of yourself and your time and everything is what we do. My husband being Pākehā doesn't understand, and says, "Don't give", and I say, "I have to. That's how I feel, that's what I need to do." He's slowly come round to that idea now. Maybe it's not leadership per se but giving makes me feel that I'm a better person in this community. When we attend a function, we always take something. We don't expect to take anything back. For me, being a good leader is looking after your community and it can happen in a range of different ways.

Leadership overlaps with service. In a Pacific community, you don't want to be seen as not contributing. When you give, you lead by example and you do this even if you know that you're going to be late with your assignment, or you know you can't get to school on time—leadership takes priority. So, if Pacific children don't turn up for school or they're late, teachers need to look at what's behind this. I'm sure it's not the child's fault—often there are things happening. Mum might have had a new baby. With Pacific children, once you get to a certain age, you're given responsibility for your younger sibling. I know Samoan teachers who were saying by the time they were 8 or 9 they were carrying a baby on their hip. That baby was now their responsibility, and then once that baby was up and walking they'd then take over responsibility for the next one coming through. That practice worked better in a village environment because you had the aunties and cousins who would help out. Usually, the eldest daughter takes on a lot of responsibility, so it's just for teachers to find out a little bit more about what's happening for the family and work out what they need to do to support these children in their learning tasks. Then the Pacific community will be thinking, "She gets it. She can understand how it is, thank goodness."

### How is leadership related to other values?

Leadership, service, and respect are all intertwined. Leadership involves service and respect. Those three things are important in any classroom, in any context. We don't talk about it; it's just how you are and how you model it and the way you do things. It's working together with others rather than barking out orders. It's working alongside and taking everyone with you—not leaving anyone behind. I do it by modelling leadership. I feel that if people see you actioning it and showing leadership, they'll use those ways as well. You know the direction that you want as a leader, but it's about guiding and leading as a guide rather than as a dictator.

### How can teachers make opportunities for Pacific learners and families to demonstrate leadership?

In terms of academic learning and achievement, there are Pacific kids who are good at maths, but sometimes they don't want to show it. They don't want to be seen as a scholar at maths, but I try and support them and encourage them that it's okay to excel in mathematics and not to be ashamed about it. They can be classroom leaders in mathematics.

There are leadership opportunities for parents who come to the school. Teachers can ask questions in a very humble way about them and their culture and what's important to them so they can know how to teach their child well. They need to ask parents, "Is there anything I need to learn? Is there anything you'd like me to know?" If grandparents are around, it would be lovely to involve them in school community events. Sometimes the teacher aides have got a huge amount of knowledge and they can also be humbly asked to share things they know about the community with the teacher. It would be great if teachers spent some more time with parents, grandparents, and others learning about their experiences and where they've come from, and what they would like for their children and grandchildren, without imposing on them. Like a teacher could ask, "Gosh, have you got any songs you'd like us to sing at mat time?" or "Would you like to have a chat to our children, and use some of your language, or tell them a story?" Teachers could make these opportunities. It's a journey for us all. We can all benefit. Teachers will have a richer repertoire of strategies to draw from, and the cultural skills can be used and adapted for a range of different cultural groups. It'll also help teachers understand that we've had to give away a lot of these things to just be here in this place—like my siblings were all fluent speakers of their language when they came to New Zealand, but they didn't use any of that language at school. How could they?

#### Example in practice: Positive behaviour management

They bell for class had rung. Students were still playing with their ball in the playground. The deputy principal was becoming increasingly annoyed that students weren't following instructions and going to class. On the way to class, a Pacific educator quietly asked the boy who owned the ball to give her the ball and walk with her to class, which he did. She gave him a way of showing leadership amongst his peers and, by removing the ball, had also removed the focus of their game. They all went off to class.

Other values present in this playground moment included inclusion and respect.

There was a cultural clash involving lack of respect for cultural ways and leadership opportunities that I saw in my own island. There was going to be big kaikai, a big feast, and so the school principal, who was Pasifika, sent the older boys out into the lagoon to get some fish for the kaikai—that was their contribution. A senior Papa'ā education adviser emailed the school to get those boys back into the classroom straight away. I thought, "Hold on, they've been swimming before they could walk. The boys weren't in any danger, they weren't swimming in the ocean, they were in the lagoon and they knew which fish they were going to get." But they went back to school and I felt that was not right. A clever teacher would have known the fishing is a good learning experience—there's maths, there's social science, there's history, geography—as well as the boys' wellbeing, because this is their contribution to the kaikai. Teachers need to know about cultural experiences so they can work out ways to incorporate the rich learning in them into their learning programmes. We've had to give away a lot of our culture and our values and so it's good for teachers to look for opportunities to incorporate these kinds of ideas and to enable these kinds of leadership opportunities at the same time.

### Are there any perceptions that undermine Pacific leadership in education?

Education is seen as the ticket to a better life by many Pacific people. There are some Pacific parents who perceive that the Western way is better than the Pacific way for education. Our language nests have been really struggling to retain our children and families, because they don't all see that as valuable education. Some mainstream early childhood centres have set up an initiative they say is a place for our Pacific communities. Mainstream early childhood policy is adhered to and fundamentally the initiative is Western-based, and the head teacher and teaching team may not be Pacific, but some Pacific people are going there rather than to the Pacific language nest, which is community based. In comparison, the language nest has less money, it's run by our mamas who sometimes don't get paid because the nest doesn't have enough money. If parents can't pay the money, the mamas say, "That's ok, next week." The perception that the Western way is better is heart-breaking because some parents cannot see how lucky their child would be to be getting her language and her sense of identity in her early childhood education—which they can do in a language nest but can't do through the kindergarten system, even though the kindergartens do a good job overall. I know parents are conflicted, because even though they see these things as really important, they want their daughter or son to do well at school and think a Western-style early childhood experience will help with that. So, their children are getting the idea at the very beginning of life that the Western way and having a non-Pacific head teacher are usual. There's still a perception that certain knowledge, Western knowledge, is more important than other knowledge, and Pacific knowledge unfortunately isn't seen as important, and this is being ingrained in these children right at the very beginning, so it's a hard battle. While this is the case, of course people are going to say, "Yes, you have your language and your culture, but it's not going to help you pass your exams. It's not going to help you get a good job." Hopefully this is changing, because Pacific cultural knowledge is increasingly being seen as important for many jobs now.

### *How do you make opportunities in your teaching for nurturing leadership?*

> *Leadership is helping learners to feel and be proud of themselves.*

Leadership is helping learners to feel and be proud of themselves. I'm always giving them praise and encouragement. I get questions like, "Miss, why do you teach maths? You're so good at maths!", and I reply, "Maths is for everybody—it's not just for the Pālagi"—in my school, there's only myself and an Indian teacher in the maths department who are not Pālagi.

Educators can make leadership opportunities in the learning environment by encouraging learners to use their initiative. If you start establishing routines at the beginning of the year, like for packing up the books and placing them nicely, it reflects in the way they set out their books—with pride. I give opportunities to explain their answers on the board; they love writing on the board—that's another way of nurturing leadership and leadership of mathematical thinking. I also encourage them to have discussions about the work, like, "Well, I got a different answer to that and this is how I did it." I think it's a bit eerie when the classroom is too quiet. I like it to have a buzz. I also encourage leadership by having them play games for learning maths for recapping ideas—games and projects are effective for giving leadership opportunities.

In lecturing, it's about ensuring students take the responsibility to do the work. I say, "I'll not chase you. You chase me if you need something." That's part of leadership, because they have to take on that role. I post a couple of reminders of what they need to do, and then get the emails, "Oh, I missed tutorial number three, what do I do?" That's shown me that most of the students have taken on that responsibility, which is part of leadership. It was through that modelling and me being patient and giving support when they asked for it. I've had to learn leadership is about them doing the work for themselves. This approach has been a learning curve for me, because when I was at home, leadership was more about telling people what to do or doing what I was told to do. How I work now has made learning a partnership, with both the students and I having leadership roles, especially for the ones I see as the naughty Pacific students who've been at university a long time without progressing—we want to get them on track earlier. We've found that putting the responsibility on the students to do the chasing when they need it has worked. I used to try and be the mother hen, chasing and encouraging them all. All I do now is provide the reminders and make sure that they've got support where it's needed.

In my leadership, I say, "Just speak up, don't be shy. Whatever you want from us, just say." It's better if we have a conversation, so we know what everyone is thinking rather than guessing. We've worked hard to put everything in place to get everyone here.

### How does someone learn to be a leader?

Starting from the bottom and working up makes you a good strong leader because then you know that once upon a time you were down there, and you understand you've earnt it.

I lead by example, as a role model. Like my Mum and Dad always said, "Go inside the house, not out here. You have to start everything inside the house before you step outside."

### How do you foster the value of leadership with learners?

I foster leadership in learners with aroha. I do this using our culture and focusing on family and our Christian values. It's also through teamwork and working here in our centre as a family—you cannot stand alone and build your castle alone. Back home, people just get up and do things, you never get told what to do. If they see something and they need to help you, they just do it and take that leadership, and it doesn't take that much effort to do it and it fosters community. When we role model this in our teaching—our children are learning those messages—they're learning the way we want them to be. When we go back home or when we live here in our New Zealand communities, this is what we expect. They're growing up with some really strong and good principles that we can show them in this place. You're passing on that wisdom to the next generation and that's a good part of leadership.

In summary, attending to the value of leadership can mean ensuring all learners are attracted to providing leadership and being led, and in their leadership, supporting them to show clarity and vision, to provide energy and renewal and build character. There are different leadership roles that can be held at different times, occasions, and contexts. Leadership is being a good role model, looking after others, having high expectations of learners, and being clear with them about these. Leadership is strongly linked to other values including service and respect.

## Discussion questions

Eta  *What are similarities and differences between the values of service and leadership?*
Rua  *How is leadership developed in Pacific communities?*
Olu  *How can educators ensure all learners have opportunities within learning environments to develop leadership qualities and skills and support their peers' leadership development?*

## Ideas for extra reading

**Living and leaving a legacy of hope: Stories by new generation Pacific leaders**
Sanga & Chu (Eds.) (2009)

This book holds a wide range of inspiring personal stories of leadership written by Pacific leaders from Aotearoa New Zealand and across the Pacific.

**Leadership learning: Aspiring principals developing the dispositions that count**
Robertson & Earl (2014)

This article discusses how principals can learn about and use characteristics and attitudes necessary for effective educational leadership towards raising the engagement and achievement of Pacific learners. The article discusses that leadership learning is emotional, social, and personal. It foregrounds how and why principals' leadership plays a role in student development and in helping students overcome the challenges and pressures they may face. Dispositions for leadership discussed include the disposition to learn; the moral purpose of working for equity; cultural awareness; the disposition to facilitate necessary change within their context; and the multifaceted nature of the leadership role in effecting change and developing capacity for change.

**O le Tautai Matapalapala: Leadership strategies for supporting Pasifika students in New Zealand schools**
Taleni, Macfarlane, Macfarlane, & Fletcher (2017)

This article discusses findings from interviews with four school principals experienced in engaging with Pacific learners. Seven areas are discussed: knowing learners and building dynamic relationships with learners and families; understanding Pacific cultural worldviews; using achievement data to inform action; using culturally responsive leadership practices; ensuring robust community engagement; holding high expectations for success and achievement; and engaging in professional development. The article discusses the key role of education leaders in ensuring that Pacific students can achieve success, as they are best placed to initiate changes and develop opportunities for underrepresented students.

## References

Fa'avae, D. (2017). Family knowledge and practices useful in Tongan boys' education. *Set: Research Information for Teachers*, (2), 49–56. https://doi.org/10.18296/set.0082

Matapo, J. J. (2017). Navigating leadership in Pasifika early childhood education: Traversing the tides of change. *He Kupu, 5*(1), 44–52. https://www.hekupu.ac.nz/article/navigating-leadership-pasifika-early-childhood-education-traversing-tides-change

Robertson, J., & Earl, L. (2014). Leadership learning: Aspiring principals developing the dispositions that count. *Journal of Educational Leadership, Policy and Practice, 29*(2), 3–17.

Sanga, K., & Chu, C. (Eds.). (2009). *Living and leaving a legacy of hope: Stories by new generation Pacific leaders.* He Parekereke, Victoria University of Wellington.

Taleni, T. A. O., Macfarlane, A. H., Macfarlane, S., & Fletcher, J. (2017). O le Tautai Matapalapala: Leadership strategies for supporting Pasifika students in New Zealand schools. *Journal of Educational Leadership, Policy and Practice, 32*(2), 16–32. https://doi.org/10.21307/jelpp-2017-0015

# Educator practice—Demonstrating and nurturing leadership

| My role | My actions |
| --- | --- |
| **Interacting with learners** | Discover the leadership roles learners hold and be understanding and responsive to these in interactions, planning, teaching, and assessment deadlines.<br><br>Give all learners opportunities to show leadership in the learning environment (e.g., classroom tasks, doing the mihi, leading the singing, group leaders, committee class representatives).<br><br>Encourage learners to demonstrate leadership through small acts of responsibility and being role models and to support others taking on leadership roles. |
| **Interacting with parents and families** | Discuss with parents their desires for their children's education and what they want the educator to know about their child and their learning.<br><br>Learn about the cultures of your learners.<br><br>Involve parents and grandparents in events and have an "Invite your grandparents day".<br><br>Invite parents or community leaders to help educators understand aspects about language or culture important for their child's learning. |
| **Planning** | Plan leadership roles and change leaders regularly.<br><br>Plan time for discussions about learning to nurture learners' confidence in their learning capability.<br><br>Plan opportunities for students to show leadership, such as through encouraging learner autonomy and sharing responsibility for teaching and learning decisions with learners.<br><br>Understand that leadership ties to other values such as service, respect, and belonging. |
| **Teaching** | Encourage learners to take responsibility for their learning and seek clarifications and to know they're always invited to ask questions when needed.<br><br>Develop a community of learners by encouraging teamwork.<br><br>Encourage everyone to understand and recognise one another's strengths and gifts and to encourage others to use these in leadership opportunities. |
| **Celebrating** | Celebrate small but important successes and acts of kindness and responsibility carried out well.<br><br>Recognise leadership through giving awards acknowledging their demonstration of the values. |

| My role | My actions |
|---|---|
| **Assessing and reporting** | Acknowledge and share ways students show leadership in the classroom and school community with parents and the leadership of the learning context.<br><br>Extend due dates for students with demanding responsibilities. |
| **Being an advocate for my Pacific colleagues, Pacific learners, and their families** | Invite Pacific community leaders to share their leadership background and journeys to leadership roles with educators and learners.<br><br>Ensure lead educators understand about and acknowledge Pacific educators' and Pacific learners' leadership activities, including their culturally linked support for the institution or leader. |

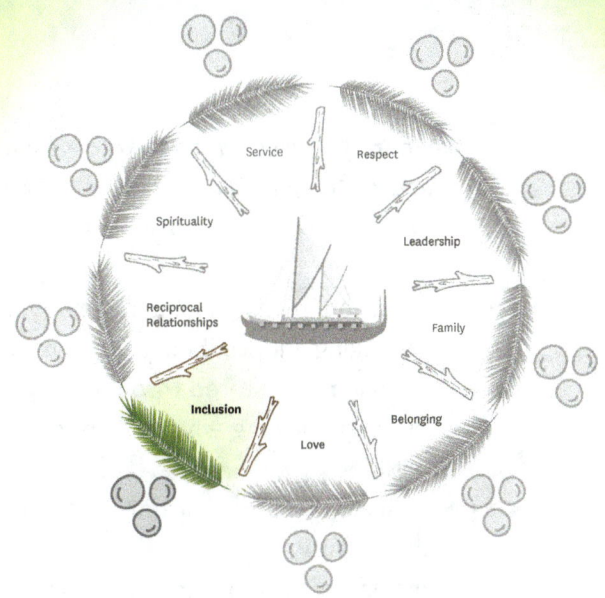

Chapter Ten

# Inclusion

**What does inclusion mean to Pacific people? How can learning environments strongly demonstrate and nurture Pacific perspectives of inclusion?**

*Pikipiki katea kae vaevae melenga*

*The Tongan proverb "pikipiki katea kae vaevae melenga" is connected to wayfinding activities within the moana. Navigating the rough open moana requires navigators to come together by connecting the main hulls of their canoes so they can share food. Manase Lua (2018) describes the proverb as "Let's link our main hulls and share everything right to the scraps! You see what's in my canoe, I see what's in yours" (n.p.). Pikipiki katea kae vaevae melenga can be linked to the spirit required within the practice of "inclusion" and resonates within the loto (heart, soul). Through the proverb, the spirit of inclusion is collectively driven and conceptualised, and requires lotolelei mo loto fiemālie (openness and willingness), faitotonu (honesty and fairness), and loto fiefoaki (generosity).*

*We thank Dr David Taufui Mikato Faʻavae, a senior lecturer in Te Kura Toi Tangata, School of Education, at Te Whare Wānanga o Waikato, for this contribution about inclusion. Malo ʻaupito.*

- Inclusion means including everyone, ensuring everyone feels belonging and wellbeing and knows that they can contribute.
- Inclusion is fostered through knowing our connections with others and knowing what is important to those we are connecting with.
- Inclusion comes from attending to responsibilities to community.
- Inclusion is celebrating languages, cultures, and priorities.
- Inclusion is using names well, communicating, and using teaching strategies that connect students with their learning.

Inclusion is making sure everyone has a part to play, everyone feels valued, and no one feels judged. Inclusion is ensuring the curriculum includes and celebrates languages, knowledge, and experiences of Pacific people and Pacific perspectives of success (Faʼaea, & Fonua, 2021; Hunter et al., 2016). Culture, community, family, and religion are foundational aspects for consideration in ensuring inclusive education for Pacific learners (Sharma, 2020; Sharma et al., 2016). Respectful reciprocal relationships are key to the success of all these factors.

Let's hear from our Pacific educators …

## *What does inclusion mean to you?*

Inclusion is having generosity of spirit. It's loving people as family and treating them as family.

Inclusive practice is seeing everyone as more than just who they are and what they can do—it connects back to that person being one of us and belonging and looking after each other. It's also how we see our elderly—they may no longer be able to operate as they would have as young, strong, fit people, but they're still part of us so we include them; we don't put them to one side, we bring them along.

Inclusion is looking out for others. It's making sure that we give as much as we can to ensure the wellbeing of this person. Inclusion is no one getting left behind. Inclusion isn't only about special needs; it's about how we're all different, but we respect the fact that you have those differences and we're still including you.

> *Inclusion is accepting the differences within our group and accepting everyone as part of us despite these.*

Inclusion is accepting the differences within our group and accepting everyone as part of us despite these. It's understanding that there'll be differences; we're a diverse group within our community, but each of us has a part to play. When I was back home in Tongareva, there was a young lady who didn't have any speech. Her task for the community was to make the kikau brooms, which are made out of the reeds and used for sweeping paths, leaves, and grass. She took her job very seriously. The day before we left, she presented us with a great big package of about a dozen brooms that she had been making in our honour. To me, that was the village looking out for something she was capable of doing, showing that inclusiveness of including people in ways they're competent and capable. We understand that everyone has limitations and that was a powerful example to me—it's looking to the strengths and goodness in everyone. There's a relaxation around how things might play out that shows understanding that no one's perfect, but everyone has something to offer.

Inclusion is knowing your connections with others and sharing these with them, so they know them too. For example, there's an old lady who's in her late 80s; every time I see her she tells me about how I'm related and how she's my mother's tuakana—although she was younger, because her mother was older. It's really important to her to tell me this—she's including me in her family 'akapapa by saying that I'm her teina because my mother was her teina. This helps you learn that you have a place—that's inclusion. With making connections, the first thing you ask is about where someone is from or who their uncle is, where their aunty is—that's inclusion. It's such a big deal to me to know my connections. When my uncle died years after my aunty did, I hadn't seen their children for a while. They mostly hadn't kept in contact with their Cook Island roots, but they felt really chuffed that I remembered their names because, since my aunty passed away, they didn't feel as if they had such a place in the wider Cook Island community. People from our islands have become really assimilated and so it's even more important that we make connections like this before they're absolutely lost. The onus is on as the FOBs, the ones who came to Aotearoa, who still have those understandings, but most of us are getting on and, once we've gone, I worry about how the connections will be continued, so we try to make sure our daughters and our sons know those connections.

One thing we do for inclusion in my family is that we all have a Cook Island name—one of our ancestors—so we can connect back our 'akapapa to the ancestors that our mothers or our grandmothers think need to be remembered. My son and my grandson are named after two of our really strong ancestors. My mum had good understanding of genealogy and she chose the names. That's an inclusive practice—knowing that, through my name, I carry my forebear with me. Those practices are also being lost as we become more Westernised, but, as a grandmother, I've named my grandchildren and I tell them about who they're named after and where they're from. Inclusion for me is making strong connections to my islands and making sure my family knows we have a right to whakapapa back to there. Language nest mamas know these names and these connections, but I think most educators in English-medium settings would never think to ask, "Where did your names come from?" However, it's such an important part of who those children are, educators can show respect to each learner by simply asking about their name, who gave it to them, and who it represents for them. It requires the teacher to be open and realise that this might be a complex conversation, because there can be a lot of connections within a child's full name. Sometimes the name is to remember a particular circumstance, like about the child's birth. People can be so proud to be given a name that has a special meaning that they go on to call their own child that name. When you give your genealogy, often it's the name and the circumstances that'll help you remember associations.

I went to a funeral a few months ago and there were a couple of special needs young men who were making a lot of noise, but they were part of the church. We don't put them out of sight. It was important they had a place there. I'm not downplaying that it can be challenging, and the family do have to rally around, but we look after each other. My mokopuna has special needs and we all take turns caring for him. If we can't do it, why should we expect other people to come in and do it? Sometimes it's hard to live like that in a Western world though when we have other responsibilities, like going to work and school and all the things we need to do to live our lives. So, we have to be cognisant that we can't always be true to these values. We don't look at anyone in a harsh way who isn't able to keep the ideals that we might have been able to operate in a village. A village is very different from how we live our lives here, and those are some of the things that we've had to give away or modify to live here, which can be difficult for those who've been born and raised with these values. Our first- or second-generation New Zealanders can often adapt more readily, but we still maintain those things that are important to us.

### How does inclusion play out in your learning context?

No children are turned away from our language nest. In our nest, there are two mokopuna who are on the autism spectrum who are really quite challenging, but they don't get turned away.

Our language nest is very inclusive; while we promote our culture and language, we honour and respect the cultural backgrounds of the families. Language nests now can have Italian, French, German speakers. We open our arms. I've asked a parent, "How do you feel about your daughter saying a lotu before they eat?", and he said, "I'm really pleased that she's able to connect to a spiritual understanding about how we bless our food." So, in my experience, anyone's welcome in our language nest. People from Europe are used to speaking more than one language and can see the benefits of this. We have space for these children because we need to make sure that we have enough children for our funding. Language nests don't fit well with a Western model; they're critiqued by the Ministry of Education and the Education Review Office because they don't tick all of the usual boxes and so Pacific people see that and think, "What's wrong with us? They're closing one down—maybe it's best to go with mainstream."

Our mamas will often teach the young parents about our values, like a cultural adviser. Their role is to make sure that children and the young parents are learning. They'll help show the parents what their children are capable of and encourage them not to do things for them that they can do themselves. They'll teach them ways to behave so that if they went back home to their village, they wouldn't be shaming their families, or wouldn't be ashamed that they didn't know what was expected. I'm sure a teacher in a kindergarten wouldn't be telling the parents off, whereas for our mamas, helping families learn is an important part of their role. With some Pacific people becoming secular, some aren't going to church or are going to modern churches like the Assembly of God, so engaging in cultural conversations in language nests is a good opportunity for them.

*How do you demonstrate and nurture inclusion in your teaching?*

Inclusion is showing that we're welcoming and that we want them to be involved. It's the kiss on the cheek, it's acknowledging them. It's sending them those connections with you. Inclusion is each child knowing that they have a place in this centre and a place in this world we live in. Inclusion's in the work that we do. We have the Pacific language weeks. We celebrate all of them. We acknowledge all of them. If we find out that a learner has an inch of connection to somewhere, we invite their parents to share something from there. It helps them to dig into their cultures and it helps us include everyone. There's a lot of intermarriage between the different Pacific groups and all heritages are important. All can be acknowledged to help foster sense of identity. My cousin has her two kids here. When they started here, she only said that the children were Niuean, Cook Island, and Samoan, but her husband is from Fiji, Samoa, and Australia. When she saw we celebrate all languages, she said, "Oh, they're also Fijian and Australian." We said, "Why didn't you say that before? That's awesome." It was really nice to be able to recognise all the children's connections.

I like to use music a lot; music, dance and drama, visual art—those are the things that I find really help with my teaching. They help with relationships and inclusion because with music, dance, and drama you see more of the person. Not all the students I've taught enjoy that stuff in the beginning, but because they see I have interest in it, by the end of the year they love it. All the parents I've spoken with so far talk about their child being a bit more confident in my class, and I know confidence helps them with everything else; they're more confident to share their ideas, and it could just be helped by a song that we've learnt throughout the year.

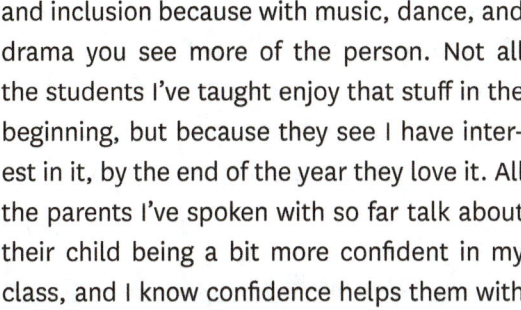

*Not all the students I've taught enjoy that stuff in the beginning, but because they see I have interest in it, by the end of the year they love it.*

### Example in practice: Developing class community

The lesson began with an inspirational video clip and learners discussing it. The educator said, "I really like this clip, why do I like this?"—the clip was about being a good friend. He made sure that everyone was included in the discussion and the lesson. Shy learners were encouraged by their peers who say, "Oh hey, come join us." Students were asked to share their writing with a friend, and to each write at least one positive comment on their peer's work. The educator told us that, at the end of every week, the class has a tribal council when everyone speaks about their highlight of the week and their lowlight. They're asked to say one positive thing about the person next to them.

Other values present in this example are belonging, love, service, respect, and leadership.

It's super diverse here with lots of different cultures and we try to celebrate all the different cultures as much as we can and so our students are not afraid to share about what they're doing at home. We celebrate difference and that's what I love about here. Also, for inclusion, I like to put responsibilities back onto them. I'll say, "You need to take ownership of your own learning. Use your initiative rather than always coming to me."

Inclusion is making allowances when life happens. If someone comes to tell me, "I've got to quarantine. My elderly grandparents are coming back, and nana has dementia and she's distressed about being in a strange place. The officials said one of us could go and stay with them. It's got to be me because I'm not married, I don't have kids." I say, "You go and do that. You go and be with them. We'll work this out. We'll have an extension." Another student was being stalked by some crazy former partner. She was stressed out asking me in tears for an extension, and I said, "Of course. What can I do to help you?"

I use names as a way of connecting and including people. I start that off by going through my roll a couple of times before the teaching begins to get familiar with the faces and the names. I have that roll with me for the whole time that I'm teaching. For tertiary teaching, it's quite hard because students aren't included in terms of our course design, but I've tried to work around that by varying their assessment options so there are original, choice-based, and creativity components. That's being inclusive by considering everybody and the skills and abilities they may have. Inclusion is trying to make learners feel at ease. Another way we do this is by having a mix of lecturers in the course with different styles—some of them easy going and some structured. In some courses, inclusion is enhanced because of the content and the way we discuss it—in one postgraduate course we have deep conversations focused on a reading and connecting it with their experiences and other things they've read. Inclusion is one of the values that I see as challenging to demonstrate and nurture in my practice as I'm not so sure what I'm doing to enhance it or how to collect evidence on this.

### What does your centre/school/institution do to demonstrate and nurture inclusion?

We demonstrate inclusion by having activities where the community comes in and interacts with the children. In our class, we also have the Niuean language, our Niuean culture that we practise, so even though English is our first language, we recognise who we are. We have our lotu, we have our prayers in our mother tongue. We do our mat time and our mother time, music, all those things that we do—not only in Niuean, but other cultures too; Samoan, Tongan, Māori are all strong in our centre. You know how they talk about the woven mat—we do a little bit of everything to incorporate everyone. We don't want to leave anyone behind.

Each learner comes with their own mentality, their own understanding, but for us teachers, we see them as one. If we do waiata, everyone sings the waiata. If we say the prayer in Māori, everyone says the prayer in Māori. If we say it in Niuean, everyone says the prayer in Niuean. It's inclusion. Everyone does everything.

We have children with special needs and we include them in everything we do even though they have some difficulties. We don't disregard their special need, but we still include them—they may have a special need but they're not incapable of doing things. If we need specialist knowledge to help a child, we get someone in to support our understanding of how to support this child. All these things come together with whatever we do in the centre. You'll find love, belonging, and inclusion coming through—they're interwoven because, if you showed love, you're making that child feel that sense of belonging and you're being inclusive by including the child. If you're not showing love, then the other two won't be showing through.

We find some students don't enjoy writing, reading, and maths but they love music and arts. Then we find their writing comes out when they're doing music and then they shine with all that learning and develop confidence in their learning because I've given them a bit of light. One girl didn't want to do anything and then she's, "Oh, I didn't even know I'm really good at writing." It would have been because of a music lesson we did. Her confidence was because we'd been able to tap into the other things that she does at home.

Our school is structured around whānau groups—that helps with inclusion. We always talk in the beginning about tuakana–teina, so seniors know about their duty to look after the younger ones, to be examples and to make sure everyone is feeling welcomed in our space. We run whānau competitions throughout the school and those things emphasise the importance of belonging, being together, and looking out for one another—all of that stuff they should be doing at home. Even the students who don't have what you would consider a normal family have this place where they feel family and inclusion.

Inclusion fits really well with how we work with the Niuean class. We try to link whatever we're doing in the unit to the Niue context. This term we're doing Matariki so we're linking to that by learning about a celebration where we do the blessing of the yam at the beginning of the year. The parents are also really good—the Niue community are quite strong together. We have meetings letting them know how the class is going. Communication with the parents and having their support for the learning at home is so important. We send out the prayer we're learning and how we're explaining, "This is what you'll hear when you go in the community and have funerals and events." Having this class is huge for us because people were getting worried they were going to lose the Niuean language. Some of the parents are New Zealand born and wouldn't have had any of the language, and the grandparents are helping children at home. We encourage the parents to help their children and then we should be able to have our language passed on. I was looking at the children today singing away and engaging—it's really nice. They say, "We're singing", and I say "You're learning. You're learning through the songs." When you hear them pronounce the words, the learning is clear, but we need resources. We have dual language books, but we need more, and we need to be given time to make resources, and we need more Niuean teachers. We're glad to have this class and hopefully the parents bring their kids into the Niuean unit to keep it going. The kids they really enjoy it. You can see their confidence. Even for the ones who are shy in class, when they're on their own we hear them, like one started singing the song in another room and I thought, "Wow!" So, we know they're all taking it in even if they're too shy to participate in class.

Sometimes Pacific children don't feel inclusion in the learning because they don't have experience of what we're teaching them about. It's interesting because they have the resources and the internet where they can search, but for many, there's a disconnect and they think, "Oh, these are just pictures. It's made up. It's not real." One of the other teachers said it's like they know with their head, but the heart doesn't understand what it's all about. We try to give them contextualised real-life learning to help.

### How can educators embed inclusion more deeply in learning contexts?

Educators knowing about names can give learners a strong sense of connection and feel included and the parents will feel their child is better understood and there's more of a relationship. They may then be receptive to inviting the teacher to important rituals and ceremonies, such as White Sunday or a big kaikai or a haircutting ceremony where their boy's going to be given another name. To me that's also inclusion, but educators have got to know something first, be keen to learn and be open and respectful.

> *Educators knowing about names can give learners a strong sense of connection and feel included and the parents will feel their child is better understood and there's more of a relationship.*

Inclusion is making sure pronunciation is correct, especially names. I really love that college students put a name pronunciation website together. Good on them for taking that initiative showing what's important and providing such a great resource. I say to our student teachers that we're all in this profession to ensure that children do well in education. Most parents have an aspiration for their children to succeed so we act on that premise. To do that, we need to find out as much as we can about our students that we don't have so much understanding of to ensure that everyone is succeeding. Some student teachers have to adjust a lot of their thinking to do this well. Sometimes Pālagi don't really understand, don't really get it and use marginalising practices and Pacific children won't always feel included by them. Education shouldn't be an endurance test of how much you can put up with. Sadly, many schools are quite marginalising for Pacific learners—they're not inclusive places for them. Sometimes teachers can have all the best will in the world but can really offend people when they make judgements from their own worldview—one told me I wouldn't be able to communicate if I cut my arms off—he meant it as a joke, but things have to change for everyone to feel inclusion and belonging. When we have a teaching force who honour our Pacific children, these children are more likely to get good education experiences.

In tertiary education, we're not making the opportunities for our Pacific learners that need to be made. We need colleagues who deeply understand, demonstrate, and nurture the Pacific values and have strong Pacific connections, and we need recognition of the strengths these people would bring. This place doesn't often have a Pacific feel but people can learn more just by having it close by, like when we had the Pacific market day with music playing and everything done in a Pacific way—making this place ours and more vibrant as well, like there would be laughter in the hallway ... Making these things happen falls on very few shoulders because we're such a small group. People will go where they feel a sense of belonging and where they feel as if they're going to be included.

In summary, attending to the value of inclusion can mean acting towards learners, their families, and the wider learning community with lotolelei mo loto fiemālie (openness and willingness), faitotonu (honesty and fairness), and loto fiefoaki (generosity). Inclusion is always welcoming and acknowledging everyone. It involves having generosity of spirit, seeing everyone as a valued part of the community—all ages and despite differences, and not leaving anyone behind. Inclusion is knowing your connections with others, looking out for how you can support others, and warmly involving community. Inclusion involves listening, flexibility, and using content, learning experiences, and teaching strategies that draw from Pacific worlds and relate to, engage, and motivate all.

### Discussion questions

Taha  *What can educators maximise inclusion in their learning contexts inclusive for all Pacific learners and families?*

Ua  *How will educators know they are successful in demonstrating and nurturing inclusion in their teaching and interactions?*

Tolo  *How can learning institutions audit and modify their policies and procedures to ensure they're consistent with the value of inclusion?*

**Ideas for extra reading**

**Moving forwards, sideways or backwards? Inclusive education in Samoa**
McDonald & Tufue-Dolgoy (2013)

This article discusses the concept of inclusive education through the Samoan context of fa'asamoa. Western thinking has influenced change in the Samoan education system. The nature of inclusive education, supports and constraints, policy and partnerships, and cultural considerations are discussed. Educator responses to policy, their partnership with families, and determination to understand why inclusive education is vital and how it can be implemented are presented as important for enhancing inclusion in learning settings.

**Making sense of inclusive education in the Pacific region: Networking as a way forward**
Miles, Lene, & Merumeru (2014)

Research focusing on the inclusion of Pacific children with disabilities in education in Pacific nations is discussed in this article which identifies that Pacific values and the role of a teacher are important for bridging learners' home and school experiences. Understanding the realities of Pacific people can lead to reduced discrimination for children with disabilities. The affordances of digital technology tools for enhancing communication and dissemination of inclusive education resources are discussed.

**Inclusive education in the Pacific: Challenges and opportunities**
Sharma (2020)

Pacific countries are becoming more active in rethinking educational policies in relation to inclusive education. This article discusses the need for increased focus on inclusive education in the Pacific, demonstrated through discussing assumptions, policies, and awareness of diverse needs and challenges to advancing inclusive education practice. Tools educators can use to enhance inclusion within their learning settings are outlined.

## References

Fa'aea, A. M., & Fonua, S. (2021). Se'i lua'i lou le ulu taumamao: Privileging Pacific notions of success in higher education. *Higher Education Research & Development*, 1–15. https://doi.org/10.1080/07294360.2021.1937954

Lua, M. (2018). *Fenua—Mana Moana session three*. https://www.leadershipnz.co.nz/blog/latest-news/2018/5/8/fenua-mana-moana-session-three

Hunter, J., Hunter, R., Bills, T., Cheung, I., Hannant, B., Kritesh, K., & Lachaiya, R. (2016). Developing equity for Pāsifika learners within a New Zealand context: Attending to culture and values. *New Zealand Journal of Educational Studies, 51*(2), 197–209. https://doi.org/10.1007/s40841-016-0059-7

McDonald, L., & Tufue-Dolgoy, R. (2013). Moving forwards, sideways or backwards? Inclusive education in Samoa. *International Journal of Disability, Development and Education, 60*(3), 270–284. https://doi.org/10.1080/1034912X.2013.812187

Miles, S., Lene, D., & Merumeru, L. (2014). Making sense of inclusive education in the Pacific region: Networking as a way forward. *Childhood, 21*(3), 339–353. https://doi.org/10.1177/0907568214524458

Sharma, U. (2020). Inclusive education in the Pacific: Challenges and opportunities. *Prospects, 49*(3), 187–201. https://doi.org/10.1007/s11125-020-09498-7

Sharma, U., Loreman, T., & Macanawai, S. (2016). Factors contributing to the implementation of inclusive education in Pacific Island countries. *International Journal of Inclusive Education, 20*(4), 397–412. https://doi.org/10.1080/13603116.2015.1081636

## Educator practice—Demonstrating and nurturing inclusion

| My role | My actions |
|---|---|
| **Interacting with learners** | Know your learners' names, strengths, and needs. <br> Pronounce names correctly. <br> Be open-hearted. <br> Invite learners to lead a song or prayer at the start of the learning time. <br> Ensure learners feel welcome and the group acts and feels like family. <br> Instil and encourage patience, tolerance, respect, and valuing of each other's differences. <br> Encourage learners to meet expectations and strive to achieve. <br> Accommodate learners' diverse life challenges. |
| **Interacting with parents and families** | Warmly invite parents to share information about their child's learning that's important for the teacher/s to know and use this information to inform planning and teaching. <br> Warmly invite parents to share with you a simple prayer in their child's family language to help their child feel included when their prayer is used in the classroom. <br> Communicate with parents about Pacific language learning examples being used with learners. |
| **Planning** | Plan content that relates to and builds on learners' life experiences. <br> Plan to accommodate learners' learning preferences, strengths, and challenges. <br> Plan learner choice into your teaching (e.g., order of content, learning tasks, ways of working). <br> Understand the role of patience, love, and respect in fostering inclusion. |
| **Teaching** | Use technology, music, art, and drama and other creative ways of learners developing and showing their learning. <br> Invite all learners to participate, ask questions, and share ideas. <br> Encourage whole-class discussion times for learners to reflect on and celebrate their learning and each other's unique gifts. |

| My role | My actions |
|---|---|
| **Celebrating** | Celebrate the Language Week of each ethnicity each Pacific child enjoys whakapapa to. |
| | Celebrate small and big successes regularly, creating a community of proud and supportive learners strong in their cultural identity. |
| | Display Pacific greetings, phrases, prayers, songs, and photographs of educators working with fanau and learners in the learning setting. |
| | Learn prayers, songs, and basic Pacific phrases together in the languages of the learners and use these with learners and fanau. |
| **Assessing and reporting** | Encourage learners to draft self-assessment and self-report comments and give feedback and feedforward on these in light of holding high, realistic expectations. |
| **Being an advocate for my Pacific colleagues, Pacific learners, and their families** | Encourage use of fanau groups that include learners from all levels and nurture inclusion, family, leadership, and respect. |

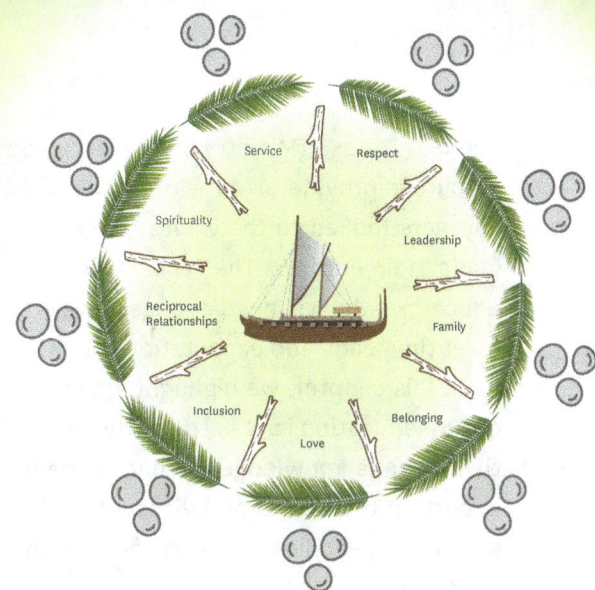

Chapter Eleven

# Honouring Pacific values: A compass for educators

Pacific children, Pacific learners, the beauty of the Pacific, are and have always been at the heart of our work. The voices in this book provide glimpses into Pacific ways of thinking about the values. The perspectives are diverse, and generalisations are not suitable. Our intentions were not to provide a definition for each value or a set of instructions of how to enact each—rather to illustrate diversity of views and provide a tool for enabling reflection and action in relation to the values.

What can we take from listening to the voices shared in this book? We can understand that Pacific values are deeply held and deeply felt. We can see that honouring the values in our interactions, actions, and teaching is vital for ensuring our learning environments are suitable and comfortable for Pacific learners and their families. We have read that relationships are key and are aided by understanding of perceptions of the values. We have learnt that taking time and effort can help us build knowledge, relationships, shared endeavour, and celebration.

However, values are but one part of what it means to be of the Pacific. While they may guide the vaka, they are not the vaka. While they may be the supporting poutu of the fale, they are not the fale. While they may provide a compass for the voyage, they are not the voyage. More is needed. *Tapasā* (Ministry of Education, 2018) and associated and other resources provide us all with further guidance and challenges. Pacific voyagers looked to the waves, the stars, the winds, birds, and sky to guide their journeys. The Pacific Values Compass is one tool we offer for educators who will need a range of ways of guiding their practice to fully meet the needs and expectations of Pacific learners and their families.

In this chapter, we highlight again why it is vital that we all work to ensure education is fit for purpose for our Pacific learners. We illustrate that there is knowledge further to the ideas in this small book that is important to uncover and discover by discussing further values important to many Pacific people. We finish with calls to action from our Pacific educators.

**Further Pacific values**

Our work focused on the nine values in the *PEP* (Ministry of Education, 2013) and *Tapasā* (Ministry of Education, 2018). However, there are further values shared by many Pacific people that are also important to understand. To illustrate that further journeying and understandings are needed, we now hear views from a smaller group of Pacific educators about four of these—gerontology, humility, generosity, and wellbeing. Consideration of wellbeing brings us back to the Pacific Values Compass and our metaphor of navigation, where we end this book and leave you to continue your journey into ways to develop and nurture Pacific values in education contexts and beyond for the benefit of our Pacific children and families. Safe and joyful journeying!

Let's hear from our Pacific educators …

*What does gerontology mean to you?*

How family and community look after our elderly is a fundamental thing. The way we care for and respect our parents and their generation shows the importance we place on our elders. We hold them in high esteem, and we celebrate that they're with us. We look to their wisdom. They have so much traditional knowledge and the language. They are our leaders. As we get older, we understand that we are starting to take some of that leadership role because we are older and wiser. We feel so fortunate to have our parents with us as our mentors. They remind us about everything they learnt before they came to New Zealand. We like to care for and look after our elderly ourselves. Family get togethers have always been a way of keeping the memories of home alive. They're living their lives as closely as they can to how it was back home and, for some younger family members, that's where a confusion can set in, as we have never expected our lives to be as much like the home countries, and as our elders have got older, they've become more traditional.

Some grandparents take a huge role in bringing up their grandchildren and this makes really strong bonds between the generations. Usually in the island way, the firstborn is given to the grandparents to raise—that happened right throughout my family so that was an expectation. My mother didn't know her real mother until she was 8 or 9 years old and people like her have traditional knowledge and authentic practices. My granddaughter spent as much time as she could with me. When I get old, I'll know that there'll be someone looking out for me. In our language nest, when children are born, they're given a responsibility for caring for one of their grandparents and as part of the Inati process (a traditional Tokelauan practice of caring for each other). It's built into their life from birth. Back home, their share of the fish goes directly to their grandparent. Teachers need to know these types of relationships can exist so they can understand the important roles a grandparent and grandchild can play for one another and why sometimes it is the grandparent who comes in to talk to the teachers when they have those connections with the children and why sometimes it is the grandparent they should contact rather than the parent.

Our language nest is right next door to the church and when the old people go to the church for a funeral during the day, the kids go and join them in the church. It's just like back home in a village—the bells are ringing in the church and they can hear the hymn, it's like being back at home. So, as much as possible, we try and have the kids help out in the church and they have the kaikai afterwards and they're part of the process with our old people; they're singing the songs and the hymns and that's powerful learning.

### What does humility mean to you?

Humility for many Pacific people is not expecting thanks but knowing what needs to be done and getting on with it. It always goes back to the roles that we play in our family. We know the roles. In our family, the matai roles are coming to younger generations and occasionally we have to remind them that, if they want our respect as the matai of the family, they know how to respect their older cousins who all have important roles. It's done in a way that's coming from a good place. Humility is making sure you don't think too much of yourself and don't think you're better than anyone else. It keeps us grounded. Having humility can be seen as a way of leading—you lead by example.

Humility, responsibility, and loyalty are connected. Humility is carrying out your role or responsibility without making everyone know it. In the Pālagi world, people generally don't know what you carry when you leave work. You can be told by the community that there's something you need to attend, and work doesn't allow for you having responsibilities that are a large part of your life. That interface can be a really hard place to be because you have to be authentic to your cultural values and the cultural ways of living your life. Decisions can be hard because I should be doing this thing because my family want me to, but I've got to do this other thing because that's my job. Constantly battling those clashes is demanding because our Western system hasn't come to terms with Pacific ways of living life yet.

Others can underestimate what is expected culturally. They can think there are church responsibilities on Sundays—well, actually there are responsibilities on Mondays, Tuesdays … it's not just church. It is great when teachers understand that some children are going to be late for all sorts of reasons, so have flexible start times for their teaching sessions that allow for children to come in when they are able to, sometimes by having a lotu ceremony at the start of the day. These things help the school be part of the community.

*What does generosity mean to you?*

Generosity is about giving—it's the giving of time, your help, financial help. Pacific people find it really hard to say no, regardless of their other commitments. In our family, generosity is important. It's how we're raised. Children learn that you give to people who need what you have more than you do, that if there's a need, and you have something, you give it without question. There's the Inati that you give everything away. I love giving. My Papa'ā husband says, "We've got to look after ourselves." No, I'd much rather give. He'll say, "Where did that thing go?" and I'll reply, "Oh my sister took it, she needed it, she wanted it." I just give, you just do.

Generosity is being a good host. When people come to visit, you make sure that they're well fed and well cared for, there's somewhere to stay, even if you've got no room, they sleep on the floor; there's things to eat even if it means spending a lot of your week's budget on it to make it nice for everyone. Your door's always open for anyone. Everyone wants to give; everyone wants to make sure that we look after everybody, that's generosity.

We show our love by giving. This can involve substantial amounts of money if it is needed by family members. An elder might say, "This is the cost for the family. Just give what you can afford to help with this cost as a gift from us", and the money arrives. With generosity, sometimes we overdo it because it is just the way Pacific people are. I always wonder if I have given enough—have I done enough? Am I looking after enough? What more can I do? Should I have given them more? Have I spent enough money? In some churches, there is an expectation of giving as much as you can give, and sometimes the amounts given are read out by family. You never look down on people, but you can wonder if you could have given more.

In our teaching, our generosity is shown through how we go above and beyond for our students and to get to know them as individuals; we're generous with our time. We make time. We understand that some learners need more from us and we give it to them.

*What does wellbeing mean to you?*

In terms of the importance to Pacific people of wellbeing, we need time to form good relationships with learners. We need to connect with what students are thinking.

The ways we live our lives—like being generous and looking after our elders—are fundamental to our wellbeing. Wellbeing is related to all of the values. We look after each other, make sure we're well fed, we're cared for to make sure we're all well.

**Calls to action**

Across this book, we have considered in some depth nine Pacific values and implications of these for educators, and we have seen glimpses of Pacific educators' perceptions of four more. The values are a navigational tool for ensuring wellbeing. Each value of the compass, each leaf, each stick, each stone has a meaning and important contribution to wellbeing. Pacific ancestors used these along with the sea, wind, cloud patterns, and stars to navigate and journey together safely; it was complex and it was skilful. They didn't rely on a machine that shows magnetic north. They needed the wisdom of our elders as guides. They were the ones who decided what needed to be done, where to go, and how to get there, and the younger ones knew to listen, learn, and contribute. To finish, let's consider further reflections, thoughts, and hopes of our Pacific educators in relation to the values and educators' work with and for Pacific learners more broadly—let's hear and let's respond to their calls to action:

> It can be such a small percentage of Pacific students who make it through the education system. Our Pacific educators and academics have been able to manage within a Western framing, but we need to make sure that all Pacific learners experience conditions that help them get through.

> One person's sense of the values will be very different to someone else's. There needs to be discussion and action to make sure all learning environments strongly enable and support the values in a Pacific sense. Such discussions need to be setting-based and institution wide —it is

not as simple as saying, 'Well if we do this, the child will have a sense of belonging', because what happens out in the outdoor spaces, at the office, in the room next door, in communication and reporting, in every part of the curriculum ... all contribute.

We hope that the ideas shared in the book can help educators work in ways consistent with the values and assist with conversations between educators and Pacific children and families—dialogue necessary for ensuring learning environments are uplifting, comfortable, and productive for Pacific people and are places where they can be themselves. Urgency is clear:

> The Pālagi mainstream thinking is different to our Pasifika way. Pālagi need to reflect our values. We've already done the Pālagi mainstream practice. They need to bring our values forward. That's their part. Our Pacific communities are important—for example, Niue, Cook Islands, Tokelau—because we're in the New Zealand realm. We're New Zealand citizens, so our Pacific values, the ways that we want our children to be raised and educated, need to be promoted so they don't lose sight of who they are as Pacific individuals. For too long, it's been a Western model that all children must fit into. There are many values and aspects of cultural identity that Pacific people share, but there are differences that we need to maintain. We need to keep hold of the essence of who we are as a Niuean or Tongan or Fijian. It's not one size fits all. There are special things about being from each island, each village, each family that we need to hold onto.

All educators need to work towards ensuring wellbeing of Pacific learners because, for our Pacific educators, learners, and families:

> It's quite tricky to be on society's margins—a lot of us are on the margins because our lifestyle isn't like the majority. We miss the village approach, which is very different. We're in isolated pockets now and we don't have our villages to go to, but we still have a hankering for the village so we create that in other ways—often it's around the church, but we've become more secular and a lot of our younger generation don't go to church. The language nests were a community-driven service run by

parents and grandparents as spaces to promote language, culture, and traditional practices, but there are so few of these and the work done in these is most often not carried through in schools or tertiary contexts.

## Discussion questions

Dua  Which ideas, stories, and pleas from Pacific educators have stood out most to you as you read this book? How will these affect your teaching and interactions with others? How can reflecting on these standouts help stimulate positive change in your wider learning environment?

Rua  Which chapter most surprised you? What surprised you in the chapter? What conversations, further reading, and professional development will you explore to deepen your understandings of the focus value of the chapter?

Tolu  The chapters of the book have explored each value in turn. What common themes have you noticed as you have read? What actions will you take personally, in your team and across your institution, that can positively impact on Pacific learners' experiences across these themes? How will you gauge your success? How will you gauge Pacific learners' wellbeing and success?

Va  Whilst cultures connect back to fundamental traditional values, cultures develop and change over time. How will you, your team, and your institution continue to stay fresh and consistent with the Pacific values as felt by Pacific learners, families, and communities of your learning environment over time?

Lima  The Pacific values are a compass, not the journey. What other learning have you identified you want to embark on to further enhance your understanding of ensuring learning environments maximise the wellbeing and achievement of Pacific learners, and the comfort and engagement of Pacific families? How will you develop this learning and how will you transfer your learning into action?

In closing, we again sincerely thank all those who have shared their wisdom, knowledge, expertise, understandings, and experiences with us in the research leading to this book and as the book has been created. To our readers, thank you for taking the time to consider the ideas shared here and all strength in using these and other learning in our collective journey of smoothing the travel for our Pacific heritage learners and their families. Thank you so very much everyone, and safe travelling on the journey, remembering that …

**O loo i lima o fanau lau tautoga o le lumanaI**
**Every child holds the promise of tomorrow**

and so,

*Now, old friend, it's time to go.*

*Our ocean-going double canoe*

*awaits us, stocked for the voyage …*

*We can delay no longer.*

(Extract from 'Tangaroa' by Alistair Ariki Campbell in Sullivan et al., 2013, p. 28)

**Pure Mutunga**

*Ka pure tātau kātoatoa*
*Let us pray together*

*Kia 'akameitaki 'ia koutou*
*Bless you all*

*Ka ma'ara'ara atu au i a koutou kātoatoa*
*I will think of you*

*Kia āru tō mātou aro'a i a koutou*
*Our love goes with you*

*Kia 'aravei viviki 'aka'ou tatou kātoatoa*
*May we meet again soon*

*Te pure nei au ki te Atua kia tiaki mai i a rātou*
*ka'aere, ē rātou ka no'o mai*
*We pray God look after those who are going and*
*those who stay behind*

*Amine*

## References

Ministry of Education. (2013). *Pasifika education plan 2013–2017*. https://assets.education.govt.nz/public/Documents/Ministry/Strategies-and-policies/PasifikaEdPlan2013To2017V2.pdf

Ministry of Education. (2018). *Tapasā: Cultural competencies for teachers of Pacific learners*. https://teachingcouncil.nz/assets/Files/Tapasa/Tapasa-Cultural-Competencies-Framework-for-Teachers-of-Pacific-Learners-2019.pdf

Sullivan, R., Wendt, A., & Whaitiri, R. (2013). *Whetu moana: An anthology of Polynesian poetry*. Auckland University Press.

www.ingramcontent.com/pod-product-compliance
Lightning Source LLC
Chambersburg PA
CBHW051149290426
44108CB00019B/2663